Follow Me

Follow Me

The Life and Adventures of a Military Family

Elizabeth Carroll Foster

hteb963@suddenlink.net

www.elizabethcfoster.blogspot.com

iUniverse, Inc.

New York   Bloomington

Follow Me
The Life and Adventures of a Military Family

iUniverse books may be ordered through booksellers or by contacting:

iUniverse
1663 Liberty Drive
Bloomington, IN 47403
www.iuniverse.com
1-800-Authors (1-800-288-4677)

ISBN: 978-1-4502-0754-6 (sc)
ISBN: 978-1-4502-0756-0 (dj)
ISBN: 978-1-4502-0755-3 (ebk)

Printed in the United States of America

iUniverse rev. date: 02/01/2010

This book is dedicated to my loving family of six who shared the fond memories and cherished photos, and to the grandchildren who share the stories with us at family gatherings: my husband John Kilby Foster Sr., our son John Kilby Foster Jr., wife Andrea, and their children Brittany Lee Foster and Evan Carroll Foster; to our daughter Lindsey Denton, her husband Vance, and her children, Benjamin Douglas Hinshaw, wife, Kelli and great-granddaughter, Rylee, to her son, Joseph Cullen Hinshaw, daughter, Amanda Lauren Hinshaw, and son Matthew Clarkson Hinshaw; to our son Steven Carroll Foster and wife Anne; to our son David Nielson Foster and wife Karen; to my late parents, Bennie and Era Carroll, my brother Franklin Carroll and wife, Naomi; and to my husband's late parents, Leonard and Mary Foster.

Finally, it is dedicated to all the military and civilian friends who made our lives more interesting along the way.

To all of those who earned my gratitude, thank you.

To my family, who prodded me to write this memoir.

To Madelyn Young of the Hot Springs Village Writers, who critiqued the final draft. To my Hot Springs critique group: John Achor, Pug Jones, Margaret Morrell, Dr. Fred Boling, Leon Harden, William G. (Bill) White, John Tailby and Danielle Burch. To my Village critique group: Madelyn Young, Gene Heath, Judy Carroll, Linda Hamon, and Mary Ann Robinson. There are others, too numerous to name, who encouraged and supported my efforts, and have earned my enduring thanks.

Memories:

> "The good things of life are not to be had singly,
> but come to us with a mixture."

Charles Lamb, 1775-1834
Last Essays of Elia. Popular Fallacies: XIII,
That You Must Love Me and Love My Dog

Adventures:

> "A harbor, even if it is a little harbor, is a good thing,
> since adventures come into it as well as go out, and the
> life in it grows strong, because it takes something from
> the world and has something to give in return."

Sarah Orne Jewett, 1849-1909
Country Byways. River Driftwood

CONTENTS

PREFACE

M ilitary life is hard for anyone who experiences it, whether of short duration or over many years.

Yet, as difficult as frequent moves, school changes, goodbyes and long separations are, it is a life of travels to places outside of one's dreams, of making new friends, and many, many fun times. It is a life of building memories to be unwrapped and relived years later. To puzzle over "what ifs," and to laugh about something that wasn't so funny at the time. It's not easy for students to change schools in mid semester, to leave friends and make new ones, but when we come together as a family, our children pull up the exciting adventures of our nomadic lifestyle and declare they wouldn't exchange it for any other.

Follow Me is not meant to be a whiner about our military life. Rather, it is the sharing of good, bad, and fun times. My husband had to deal with my collection of parking tickets. We traveled across the United States, lived in Pakistan, toured in India and Italy with four youngsters and a dog. My brother drove the old Blue Bomber up on an airstrip. My first airplane ride was with a new baby dosed for teething. Four babies were born in five years. I cracked the door to a love-making scene. Listened to bliss and bed rhythms of a newlywed couple. We dealt with our loveable dog's mishaps and the breakdowns of our faithful old car. Along with my husband's achievements in a thirty-year career, all of the above made for an exciting life.

John volunteered shortly before World War II ended and spent sixteen months in military service. We married in 1949, and he was recalled to service in 1950 at the outbreak of the Korean War. The second interruption of his education was a big factor in his decision to make a career of the military.

A year in Korea and two in Vietnam meant long separations for our family. Wherever my husband was stationed, temporary duty (TDY) assignments were frequent. We lived two years in Pakistan, where John flew U.S. civilian engineers from Karachi to project sites in the north. He was chosen for test pilot training at the U. S. Naval Air Test Center, Patuxent, Maryland, then was reassigned there as a helicopter test pilot. When the navy stint ended, we moved to Edwards Air Force Base, California. There, at the Army Test Center, he performed aircraft tests for more than four years. At Edwards, he broke the Russian speed record in a helicopter. John retired in 1975 as project officer for the Federal Aviation Administration. At the time, we had lived in Camp Springs, Maryland more than six years.

After twenty-five years as the spouse of a U. S. Army officer, I think I know a thing or two about military wives. They are full of grit.

Military wives have much in common, regardless of the branch of service. Conditioned to be strong, they show endurance even when a hard life gives them a good smack. Then, they might sit down and cry. But not for long. There is always another move to make, another house to turn into a home. Another goodbye to a husband and friends. More explanations to children that their dad will not be home for a birthday, a special award ceremony, Thanksgiving, Christmas, or a graduation.

Astute at bringing understanding to children who leave old friends behind and face making new ones, military wives are community volunteers and social beings. Through it all, they keep households sane, kids corralled, and welcome husbands home with a smile. They are wizards at explaining a father's death. During tragedies, they share food, tend the deceased's children, and put the house in order for a grieving friend. They grieve together in bad times and laugh together in good times.

Military wives accept the life that's dealt them.

Such are the stories that fill this book and allow me to relish the retelling of them.

HAD I KNOWN, WOULD I?

The morning after John left for Korea in December1952, I stood before the mirror. It reflected a dazed gaze. Dark circles ringed the eyes staring back at me. Listening to Aunt Viola in the kitchen, talking to Johnny as she made his breakfast, and knowing our six-day-old daughter was finally asleep, I wondered how I would manage when John's aunt was no longer with us.

"Brace yourself, kid," I muttered to the mirror image. "You have a twenty-month-old and a six-day-old baby dependent on you alone, and you will not fall apart today."

Had I known the twist our life would take, would I have made a marriage commitment? Would I have borne children?

On September 6, 1949, I became a bride, and was clueless as to what lay ahead of my groom and me in less than a year.

Earlier that year on a June evening, John and I sat on my parents' front porch. "I'm leaving in September for Oklahoma." His matter-of-fact announcement that soon he would be heading off to the University of Oklahoma spurred me to action.

I turned to him. "Wish I were going with you." That was as close as I could get to a proposal without making it outright.

"Will you?" That was as close as John could come to proposing.

"Yes." And just like that we were engaged. We set the date and had less than three months to question a commitment or to back out all together. We had "gone steady" for three years, surely enough time to work on commitment. If either of us thought of backing out, we didn't mention it. Months passed with a series of wedding showers.

September 6 arrived. I sat at the dining table polishing my nails and second-guessing why this task occupied me. I didn't care for polished nails, preferring them in their natural state. Was this my way of foot-dragging on the way to the altar?

From the doorway, Mother fussed and Aunt Nelle urged, "Time is running out, Elizabeth. You must get dressed." They prodded, while Dad, never one to get too involved in any kind of turmoil, stayed out of the fray. We arrived at the church minutes before three o'clock.

With the fifteen-minute ceremony over and a handful of rice thrown, John led me across the street to the courthouse, where the county clerk, Joe Rhodes, recorded our marriage date. Now, I thought it would have been recorded anyway, but John wanted to be sure.

Back at the church, we drove away in his parents' new '49 Dodge purchased before they gave the old "Blue Bomber" to us.

The 1937 Plymouth, painted sky blue, was our dating transportation for three years. The day before our wedding, we had packed the back seat, the back floorboard, and trunk with gifts and clothing—everything we owned jointly. John stowed the car in his parents' garage. "There won't be any writing on this car or tin cans tied to the bumper," he had said.

His natural shyness prevailed when my instinct had been to shout to the whole wide world, "I'm getting married tomorrow."

After the wedding, we said goodbye to his parents, backed the Bomber out of the garage, made a short stop to say farewell to my parents and aunt, and began a journey that would lead us from pillar to post for the next twenty-six years.

BEWARE OF BUMPS IN THE ROAD

John's intention was to pursue two years toward a petroleum engineering degree at the university. Until now, my parents had borne most of the unhappy times, leaving me to live a happy childhood and youth. Now, one month away from age twenty-one, I was about to take up a life of great happiness and much loneliness. Looking back, three events occurred on our wedding day that should have been a foreshadowing of the bumpy ride ahead.

We left our hometown on the first of a lifetime of adventures together without a hint at the pattern our life would take. We had gone twenty miles in the Bomber, when we heard "blump, blump, blump." John pulled onto the highway shoulder. "The car has a flat tire." In suit and tie, my handsome knight hauled himself out of the car, removed the tire and replaced it with the spare. Soon we were off again without a thought to where we would spend our wedding night. Probably some roadside motel along the way.

Not to worry. My husband had everything under control.

Twilight approached as we drove away from the Texarkana service station with a repaired tire. The first forewarning was behind us, and we threaded our way westward toward the outskirts of town. As we exited the city limits, fate intervened a second time. The Bomber's headlights failed, and we turned back to the service station. It was closed.

"We'll stay at the Grimm Hotel and get the lights repaired in the morning," John said.

Holey-moley! My senior prom was held there, at which time I had declared, "I will not spend my honeymoon here." It was a grand old hotel, but the name was enough to cast despair.

I was mortified at such a prospect, but there we stood in the hotel lobby, facing two attendants behind the check-in counter. They gave each other knowing nods. "Uh-huh, newlyweds." My corsage and John's boutonniere were dead giveaways.

A bellboy led us to a fourth-floor room resembling nothing of modern-day hotel decor. The Grimm Hotel didn't have air-conditioning. It was practically unheard of in 1949. The night presented a hot time in the old inn. What did I step into in this marriage deal? One look at John gave the answer. For better or worse.

After breakfast the next morning, we drove to the service station for the headlight repair. "A voltage regulator replacement," the service person said.

The flat tire, Grimm Hotel and faulty regulator behind us, we pulled away from the station. I was confident my husband knew how to get things done. He could and would take care of me. With my sense of security intact, we sped off into a new morn that promised to be as hot as our Arkansas wedding day had been.

Zipping along, fresh air poured through the car's open windows, cooling our faces. At noontime, we drove into the city of Paris. Texas, that is. "What's better than part of our honeymoon in Paris?" John asked over lunch in a Paris café.

What honeymoon? I thought, giving him a weak smile.

Leaving that fair town, we saw the last tall pine trees, so familiar to our southern Arkansas environment, disappear. Soon, there was a different lay of the land, where the elevation reached more than eight hundred feet around Ardmore, Oklahoma.

It was late afternoon and the sun dropped behind the horizon when John entered a parking lot parallel to a cluster of World War II Navy barracks. Home to married students.

Wind whipped long hair across my face as we lugged boxes over to one of the buildings.

Our corner apartment, located on the back of a long two-story structure, consisted of two rooms on the lower floor. We walked into a room furnished with a couch that made into a bed, a chest of drawers, one chair, and a tiny closet with fabric-draped closure. Adequate, I thought, moving to the next room. Cabinets, cooking range, and a small table with four chairs outfitted the kitchen. "Hm-m. Rust stains in the sink." I pulled one of the chairs from beneath the table, sat down and mumbled, "Okay."

John entered with another load from the car.

"Where's the bathroom?" I asked.

He stood in the doorway between the two rooms, sending me a sheepish look. "I forgot to tell you. We share shower rooms with others in the building. I think females are upstairs. Guess males are downstairs."

Remembering gym shower rooms in the El Dorado and Houston schools I had attended forced a grimace.

With everything unloaded from the car and lying in piles on the couch and floor, we sat down to our first meal. A can of Campbell's Chicken Noodle Soup. I never told John I couldn't cook, but I had confidence that a *Betty Crocker Cookbook* would solve that problem.

The next day, we bought food supplies, the cookbook and a small refrigerator.

As September slipped into fall, I learned to avoid peak hours in the shower room. And to tolerate odors that saturated the apartment, clothing and my hair with scents of onion and other concoctions I made. Oklahoma weather proved too frigid to open windows.

Days passed, and John discovered I cleaned like a fanatic but knew nothing about starching clothing. I brought two of his white shirts from the clothesline and stood them on the floor before him, awaiting his comment.

His face wore astonishment. "What did you do?"

"I starched them." A few days later, I trekked back to the laundry room, convinced my housewifely role presented hard-learned lessons. It wasn't funny then, but looking back, a mental picture of the shirts standing on their tails like two defiant dwarfs, brings a chuckle.

One afternoon, an upstairs neighbor invited me for a visit. An art student, her idea of home decor was painting her walls black. Her apartment resembled a bat cave.

Sometimes alone in the building, the radio amused me while I tried to knit a pair of argyle socks for John. They didn't pass the muster. I played newlywed tricks on my husband when he returned from classes. Listening for his approach, I hid in our tiny closet or behind the door and peeked at him through the crack. He walked back into the hallway, looking up and down. I could see John wasn't the least bit worried. It was his way of playing into my game.

I tested my culinary skills on the couple across the hall. Their names escape me, but she came from Cody, Wyoming. Her husband, a native of The Netherlands, attended the university and sold jewelry to supplement her pay from a job on campus. Later, when I had to apply for a job, she helped me obtain the position of secretary to the head of the University Physical Department, which maintained buildings and grounds. On this evening, with the help of my cookbook, I served them baked ham dressed in pineapple slices and brown sugar.

Trusting Betty Crocker, we invited David Clary, John's friend from Magnolia A&M College and also a student at OU, to dinner a number of times. David's family lived eight miles east of our hometown, and he had made a Thanksgiving trip to Arkansas in the Bomber with us. At Christmas time, he was hospitalized and couldn't make the trip home. Badly burned in a dorm fire, he had jumped from his second floor window. His mother and brother came to Norman to visit him. I invited them for a pot roast dinner and winced with embarrassment over that meal. Instead of consulting the cookbook, I tried Mother's method, but it didn't turn out like hers.

After Christmas, I applied for the secretarial opening at the University Physical Department and passed the typing and dictation tests. The pay couldn't have been much. But we had enough with John's GI bill, his National Guard stipend, and my pay check to buy food and gasoline, pay the rent, take in a weekly movie and even afford visitors.

My brother drove our parents to Norman, and we solved sleeping arrangements by renting empty apartments in our building. Both our mothers were wonderful cooks, and I felt intimidated. The cookbook got a real workout during their visit.

We didn't have much of a social life, but it wasn't necessary for our well-being and happiness. The Blue Bomber took us where we needed to go, and we didn't have a worry in our world until notification came that the barracks buildings where we lived were to be razed.

With rental ads in hand, we headed out to look for a place to live. Shown a garage apartment with three rooms, hardwood floors, a bath all our own and rooms nicely outfitted, I was hooked.

"Can we afford it?" John drove around the neighborhood streets as we debated that question. "Fifty-four dollars for rent would take a large chunk out of my GI Bill allowance." John had volunteered in the Army Air Corps in 1944, served sixteen months, was discharged but remained in the military reserves. When the three-year reserve period ended at the university, he joined the Oklahoma National Guard. His GI allowance amounted to one hundred twenty dollars a month, the National Guard allotted thirty-five dollars a month, and there was whatever my job paid.

The rent was out of our league, but I wanted that apartment. "We can swing it, one way or the other."

Returning to the landlord, we rented the place.

Ah-h, to be young again. Life at the university was a bowl of cherries, even if we rolled around in Erma Bombeck's pits. We were learning lessons of survival when our plans to spend two years at the university were suddenly changed.

After five months in the barracks and seven in the garage apartment, the "Finger of Fate" struck. Erma's pits hadn't prepared me for the destiny ahead.

Kismet took charge of our lives during the summer school break in 1950 with outbreak of the Korean War. Our world turned topsy turvy, and I wrapped our first together times in happiness and crammed them in my memory box. Over the years, we've taken out those memories, unwrapped them, and had a good laugh.

YOU'RE IN THE ARMY NOW

*L*ife as a military wife wasn't on my scope when we married. Our life together had been innocently happy, so how in heaven's name did we land in a pit of war? The answer to that question was soon to become clearer. My husband was more prepared for what lay ahead of us than I.

When John volunteered in the Army Air Corps in 1944, he expected to have flight training. He left in May 1945, a week before his high school graduation, to fulfill his volunteer commitment, War with Germany wound down and ended in April 1945. Around that time, flight training programs were phased out even though the Japanese were obstinate and war continued. John ended up in the Army Air Corps ground forces. He finished basic training at Sheppard Field in Wichita Falls, Texas and qualified for Cryptographic Technician School. He was sent to Scott Field, Illinois. When cryptographers were no longer needed, he volunteered to be a Control Tower operator at Scott Field. The war with Japan ended, and he was discharged in September 1946 after serving sixteen months and twenty-one days. Along with his military discharge came a required commitment of three years in the Armed Forces Reserve.

Again a civilian, John entered and completed two years at Magnolia Agricultural and Mechanical College in southern Arkansas, where he took flying lessons and earned a private license in a Piper Cub.

That was his military and college history before we married and arrived at the University of Oklahoma.

Soon after we landed at the university, his three-year Reserve commitment ended, and John enlisted in the Oklahoma National Guard. "My control tower experience will serve me well, for I was assigned radio operator duty for the Guard's aviation section. This will increase our coffers by thirty-five dollars a month. Guard meetings are four hours long on two Saturdays a month. They're held in an abandoned Navy hangar near our apartment." He softened his re-connection with the military as much as he could.

Meetings and nearness factors weren't unreasonable, I thought, and the extra money shouldn't be discounted. But, had we suspected that extra thirty-five dollars was to change our lives, perhaps we would have made a different choice.

During the summer break from classes, John took a temporary job with the University Physical Department. He mowed a lot of grass. Most evenings, we listened to radio news of the Korean Conflict. It loomed as a concern but didn't touch us personally. After all, it was said, "We'll go over there, whip 'em and be home by Christmas." That he might be called back into service never occurred to me.

Then, the crack of doom wiped out our future plans in an abrupt manner in mid 1950.

It suddenly became a serious issue in July, when John called my office. "The Forty-Fifth Division Thunderbirds are being called to active duty. I'm being recalled for military duty."

Being recalled for active duty! What did the Forty-Fifth Division have to do with my husband? "What does that mean?" I asked. What did I know about the connection between the National Guard and the Forty-Fifth Division?

He explained that his National Guard aviation section belonged to the Forty-Fifth. "I'm being recalled into military service," he reiterated.

"How could this happen?" Perhaps I thought Guard duty was something like the state police. Except different.

Without models, I had no idea of an army wife's role, or how a family could be raised under those conditions. My first thought was, What if I am pregnant?

My knowledge of the military came from World War II movies and newsreels. Back then, soldiers weren't encouraged to marry and the bulk of U.S. forces was made up of single men. Newsreels in movie theaters had more often shown Gold Star Mothers receiving word of sons lost in the war. While I knew several wives who lost husbands, it didn't seem overwhelming numbers were publicized.

Whether or not I was knowledgeable of the role, I was about to become a military wife. It was all the more difficult to accept for we had been taking my temperature nightly to determine ovulation time in an attempt to get pregnant. Now, the primary sign made me suspect we were successful.

Within the next two weeks after John phoned the office with news of his recall, I overcame the stunning blow and tried to accept the fact that I was to be an Army wife.

Soon the dreaded time of our first separation arrived. John sat behind the wheel of the Bomber, ready to drive me to Arkansas. Again, all of our belongings were stashed in the back and trunk of the car. Our landlord and his wife stood nearby, wishing us good luck. One of them said, "Elizabeth, we want you to return and stay with us until John leaves for Camp Polk"—the Forty-Fifth's destination.

Well, that put a brighter light on our situation. "Thanks. I'll consider it, depending on how long he remains here."

John dropped the Blue Bomber and me at my parents' home and flew back to Oklahoma to help prepare his unit's move to Camp Polk, Louisiana.

With boxes stashed and clothing hung in the closet, I settled into my former bedroom. Two weeks passed with my family, then I boarded a slow train back to Norman. Upright for thirteen hours on the passenger car wooden bench didn't seem much of a sacrifice to make to be with my husband. The monotonous "clickety clack" of wheels on rails led me to contemplate how long I would have with him. Should I tell him I might be pregnant?

Our former landlords welcomed us into their home, where she operated a hair salon. I took on the tasks of shopping for food, preparing dinners for the four of us and cleaning the house. Morning sickness, tiredness, all the symptoms mingled with the joy that I might be headed for motherhood. My feelings edged onto something hard to describe, but the overriding one was that I might not be with John to share our first child's birth.

Each day I moped around, imagining what life would be without him. Each evening, his arrival brought treasured time together. Alas, the morning came when our host drove me to the train station and waved as I left on the arduous, thirteen-hour train ride back to my parents.

The next two weeks of waiting for John's move to Camp Polk passed slowly. I had yet to mention my suspected condition to him or my family, because I wanted the doctor's confirmation. When I did tell Mother, she said, "I knew it all along."

I wondered what my school friends would think about me being pregnant. Jokingly, I had vowed to them that I would have triplets and name them Dirk, Kirk and Mirk. They had laughed and said, "Yeah, that'll be the day when Elizabeth Carroll has kids."

Gosh, those had been carefree days. Now, miserably lonesome for my man, I yearned for those fun times so recently left behind. I didn't know then, but that kind of fun was never to be recaptured, and I had some growing up to do. My future held years of learning how controlling and demanding the role of a military wife could be.

A life of separations lay ahead of John, our future children, and me.

THE SIGNS READ, "FOLLOW ME"

John arrived in Louisiana and called a few days later. "I've found a place for you." Sounding happy, he warned, "Don't get too carried away. People are renting chicken houses to servicemen. We're lucky to get rooms in DeRidder, a town twenty-six miles from the base."

Excitement kept me from hearing much of what he said. Suddenly, he blurted, "Listen for a minute. You have a bedroom and will share the bath in a five-room mill house. It's nothing to brag about, but the best I could do. Found it through the Chamber of Commerce."

"Don't fret, I can live any place as long as I'm with you," I said, remembering a recently shared restroom and shower.

The next day, my brother and I rose at five a.m. to get an early start to Louisiana. I don't know how far we had gone over a route Frank chose through backwoods country, when he pulled the Blue Bomber to the side of the highway. "Why are you stopping?" I asked.

"Don't you know the gas tank in this car has a leak? Don't worry, I have a bar of soap. I'll rub it into the crack, and that'll hold it for a few miles."

"Why didn't you tell me?"

"I didn't want to worry you." Did he suspect I was pregnant?

With the leak plugged, we remembered our plan to stop along the way for breakfast. Soon we crossed the state line, and ahead I spotted a restaurant sign. "Let's stop there."

Slowing, Frank steered even with the eatery. "It doesn't look clean," he said, driving past it, and I feared my nausea would add more delays to stopping to soap the gas leak.

Speeding along, the August air through open windows blasted our faces with heat. We passed into and out of the town of Alexandria, and I checked the map. Another twenty miles and a number of soap stops later, we came upon periodic yellow signs, bearing a thunderbird, the totem pole-style insignia of the Forty-Fifth Division. It had beckoned the moving convoys to Fort Polk, and now it beckoned us. The signs' messages read, "Follow Me."

Frank followed the signs to an open gate and guardhouse. Overhead another sign announced: Camp Polk. "This is it." He stopped the car. "Should we go in?"

"I don't know. What do you think?" I looked about. Our only experience on a military facility had been when Dad drove us through Barksdale Air Force Base near Shreveport when it was under construction. In the movies, military posts were always depicted with high fences and guards on the gates. "There isn't a guard, and I don't see a 'Do not enter' anywhere."

Frank eased the Bomber through the tumbled-down gate, past the vacant guardhouse and down the canyon-like road through the thick pine forest. Poking along in nervous anticipation of what could happen, he asked, "What if soldiers come out of the trees with drawn rifles and bayonets? What if they order us to halt? Or worse yet, throw us in …what's the jail called in the Army?"

Without a clue, we traveled alone over the road for what seemed like miles. Finally, forest gave way to buildings and men garbed in olive drab uniforms. Frank drove down streets without knowing the direction we should take to find John. Suddenly, we came upon an impressive building sited on a slight rise. In front, a sign read: 45th Infantry Division Headquarters. "Turn in here," I pointed to a circular drive. Frank stopped at the entrance steps.

The possibility of a car pulling up behind the Bomber and the commanding officer demanding to know why we were parked there didn't occur to Frank or me. My only thought was, the headquarters had an air of importance. "If anyone knows where John is, they should." I stepped from the car and went inside. Following the red carpet to a large desk, I stood before a young soldier.

Looking up with apparent amazement, he said, "Can I help you, ma'am?" I explained my husband was on the base, but I didn't know how to find him. "What outfit is he in, ma'am?"

"I don't know. He was in an Air National Guard unit at the University of Oklahoma when called to service."

"He's probably over at the airfield." Turning to others behind smaller desks, he got agreement and gave directions. "You go straight down this street out front, cross the railroad tracks and turn left at the warehouses. You'll see the airfield over there."

Back in the Bomber, we turned at the warehouses and stopped. We didn't see an airfield. Only trees loomed ahead, but soldiers worked around the warehouses. "I'll ask them how to reach the airfield," I said.

"That-a-way." One pointed. "Go behind this building; there's a dirt road back there. Leads right to the airfield."

Frank turned back and headed down the dirt road. Shortly, the little-used road, appearing to be no more than a wagon path, came to a dead-end at a two-foot high embankment. Stopping in front of the gravelly roadblock, Frank looked exasperated. Leaning his lanky frame over the steering wheel, he said, "That's the field. See the windsock?"

Before I could think, he backed up, threw the Bomber into first gear and sped up the embankment. Tires spun, gravel projectiles shot in all directions and dust fogged our view. When the air cleared, a helmeted man in uniform came running toward us, flailing his arms overhead. A rifle hung from his shoulder and bounced at his side. "What are you doing? Get off the runway! That way," he directed.

I was so nauseated, it was difficult to raise my head, but I did and recognized the soldier. It was my John.

Frank obeyed and parked the car.

Having ordered us into submission, John asked, "Why in the world did you come that way? You drove onto the airstrip."

Our goofy arrival in front of comrades and his commanding officer was embarrassing, but to this day, my husband has never shared the ribbing they must have given him.

Later in the day, as John drove us to my new living arrangements in DeRidder, we told him about entering the base through an unguarded, back gate. He eased our fears. "Only convoys watching for the 'Follow Me' signs would come through the back gate. That's the reason you were out there alone. What route did you take to wind up there, anyway?"

That was a good question.

FIRST MILITARY HOME BULGES WITH PEOPLE AND HARBORS ROACHES

Having made a foolhardy landing on the airstrip, my brother's first words to my husband were, "Sis is real sick. She hasn't eaten anything, and we need to get her some place for food." At the time, John was a private first class. Most likely, he had eaten humble pie when he asked his commanding officer for permission to take us for food then drive on to my new home in DeRidder. His superior agreed, and off we went to the enlisted men's canteen. Inside, John ordered sandwiches and returned to the Bomber. August sun beamed down on Louisiana and the car as we ate. I felt the heat and pimento cheese combination wasn't going down well.

Finished with lunch, we left the post and pulled into a Leesville service station for gas before hitting the road to DeRidder, twenty-six miles away. While the car was serviced, I ran inside to the restroom and rid myself of the sandwich eaten only minutes before. Returning through the station, I noted a sign over the door: Greyhound Bus Station. Maybe that accounts for the filthy restroom, I thought.

Back in the Bomber, I lay across the back seat, feeling as "weak as a rained-on-bee." Suddenly, I raised up and blurted, "I must have a Coke right now, or I'm going to die!" Frank rushed to the ice-filled drink box in front of the station and returned with a Coca Cola in a six-ounce, green bottle. Nothing ever soothed so much, and I asked for another one.

Having downed two drinks, the nausea subsided, and we started for the small Louisiana town that was to become my first home as a military wife.

John rolled the car to a stop in front of a white frame house. A woman with straw-colored hair, freckles, and blooming in her own pregnancy greeted us. "The back door is closer to your room." She pointed the way around the house. "Drive to the back and I'll meet you there. Come with me." She indicated me. I followed, and at the kitchen door, she invited, "Come on in." Holding screen door open for Frank and John to enter, the woman introduced herself.

She led us into a bedroom behind the kitchen. This will be your room. All of us use the bathroom over there." Mrs. Flint pointed across my room. "Two doors lead into it. Yours and ours' from the hall. When in there, you must lock both doors, and we'll do the same." She continued. "We rented the living room to another young couple. They will be here Sunday," Her mouth formed a thin-lipped smile. "I have a husband and three-year-old daughter. Maggie sleeps in our room."

We got the picture. The house would soon bulge with people. I didn't understand then, but anytime the military invaded small towns, the sudden influx of people overwhelmed the communities' abilities to provide adequate housing, streets and schools.

Mrs. Flint paused long enough for me to introduce John and Frank, and give my name. Concerned about where my brother would sleep that night, I asked, "Is there a hotel in town?"

"How long is he going to be here?"

I gave Frank a questioning look, and he said, "I have to leave tomorrow."

"Oh well, in that case, he can sleep on the fold-out couch in the front room. Now, I'll just go clear some space in the pantry for your kitchenware."

She left us standing in the bedroom and looking dumbfounded at each other. I tried to visualize the layout of the place. Following her from the front of the house, we had passed from the living room, soon-to-be another couple's bedroom, into a narrow dining room, then into the kitchen. I noticed an open door from the dining room into a hallway. A mental picture of the bathroom we would share formed. It must be halfway the length of my bedroom. My small closet took the remainder of that wall. How long will I have to live like this? I wondered.

John's face showed self-doubt, as though asking, "Did I make a mistake by renting this place sight-unseen?" He overcame apparent guilt with an explanation. "I must be back at the base by midnight. Enlisted men can leave Camp Polk at four o'clock each afternoon, but must return in the middle of night." Time moved on, and he looked at my brother. "Frank, help me unload the car."

They walked out and I stood glued to the spot, trying to get past my husband's restrictions and my new living conditions. Were Camp Polk and DeRidder, Louisiana, on God's observation screen?

Returning from the car with a load of clothing, John must have seen disappointment in my face. He gave me a hug and reassured, "We'll have weekends together, too."

Frank brought the last boxes of linens and kitchenware from the car, and by this time, I was feeling hunger pains. "I saw a store about half a block up the street. Do you think we could get a snack?" He and John returned from the store with Cokes and Baby Ruth candy bars. The bedroom had no chairs, so all three of us sat on the bed savoring treats and laughing at our predicament.

"It's good we came upon Camp Polk when we did." Frank laughed. "I was running out of soap." We told John about the leak and stopping at the headquarters building for directions, and other events of our day. Appearing flabbergasted, he shook his head.

We had laughed until giddy, when John glanced at his watch. "It's close to five-thirty. Think we ought to find a place to eat?" I located Mrs. Flint and asked about a restaurant.

In a small downtown café, we ordered "home-cooked" meals. It was still daylight when we finished dinner and stopped at the bus station to check the schedule. Frank's departure time was seven a.m. with a transfer in Shreveport to a bus going north.

Back at the Flint house, he retired early, and John and I sat on our bed until he left for Camp Polk around eleven p.m.

The next morning, voices from the kitchen woke me. Mrs. Flint said she had seen her husband off to work and she and little Maggie were having breakfast. The child was adorable. Her freckles and reddish-brown curls reminded me of Shirley Temple.

Our new landlady pulled open the closet door and pointed to a deep shelf. "You can put your kitchen things here."

When she and Maggie left the kitchen, I removed pots, baking pans, serving dishes, and tableware from boxes, washed them and filled my assigned space. Then I walked across the street to the small grocery and returned with crackers and canned soup. At lunchtime, I waited for the kitchen to be vacated before thinking of warming a cup of soup. Opening the closet door sent a hoard of monster-sized roaches scurrying over my clean kitchenware. Hunger slipped away. I closed the door in dread of having to wash everything again.

The new couple arrived to set up in the living room, and it was harder yet to get a turn in the kitchen. The only full meal we ate was on a Sunday evening when all the other dwellers were away. We broiled steaks. To stay ahead of the roaches, I survived on meals from the little store—lunchmeats, Pork 'n Beans, crackers and peanut butter.

Another young military wife lived next door under similar conditions. She baked an apple pie and invited me for dessert. While appreciating her gesture, I imagined roaches running across the plate.

The Flints were kind enough, but after two weeks, John and I answered a newspaper ad. The door to a large white, two-story house opened to an elderly gentleman. His kind face and rotund belly resembled our aged, family doctor, recently deceased in our hometown. After introductions, Mr. Nichols led us to a rear, sitting room where his wife waited. Gray hair pulled into a rolled bun on the back of her head and her ready laugh rekindled memories of my maternal grandmother.

We rented one of their upstairs, one-room apartments. In a corner, cabinets hung above and below the kitchen sink. A small cook range and table with two chairs completed the kitchen area. A bed and two overstuffed chairs made up the rest of the furniture. A bath down the hall was shared with another military couple and anyone who later rented a third upstairs room.

Mr. Nichols cleaned the stairs, landing, hallway, and bathroom each morning. His wife, crippled by arthritis, left the cleaning to him, but she managed to cook their meals. She made tasty turnip greens, and sometimes sent her husband upstairs with a serving for me. But, oatmeal cookies were her specialty, and she often invited Betty, the other military wife, and me to her sitting room for treats with coffee.

Louisiana coffee required a cultivated taste for chicory. I wasn't prepared, but managed to drink it without offending the gentle lady's hospitality.

Living conditions improved with the elderly couple, and I no longer dreaded the time John would spend at Camp Polk. Too, I had a future event to think about. A local doctor had confirmed my suspicions. "You are pregnant."

One day Betty wanted to go downtown. She didn't drive, and John and her husband, Bill, had gone to the base in the Blue Bomber. So, we walked into town despite the summer heat.

In the drugstore I leaned against a counter, waiting for Betty to make a purchase.

Suddenly, slipping into an unconscious state, I slid to the floor. My head bent mere inches from my spread legs and a wet towel was held to my forehead when my eyes opened.

A gracious stranger drove us home.

Sometime during this period, I remember vaguely, the airfield commander's wife called wives together in her home. "You need to buy a copy of *Army Wife* and read it," she advised. I bought the book and learned what was expected of a military wife. Be sociable, entertain, volunteer, support your husband, do not show weakness with tears when you part but leave him with a smile to remember, …

We made one trip from DeRidder to visit our parents in Arkansas. "I don't know how you live as you do," Mother said. "When Frank returned from taking you down there"—she meant Louisiana—"he said, 'Poor Sis, I don't know how she's going to live like that.'"

She seemed relieved when I told her life was much better with the Nicholses.

For years after our sojourn with them, I sent seasonal cards to the elderly couple. Then, one Christmas a note from their daughter stated both were deceased. Some people just make all the difference in the world. Indeed, the kind old couple enriched our lives.

Our time with them was short. In November, news came of John's selection for Officer's Candidate School. But first he must attend Leadership School at Fort Jackson, South Carolina. This was good news, for if not OCS, he would go to Korea.

It was time to start on another adventure.

WE CAN AFFORD THE APARTMENT
IF WE SHARE THE RENT

We said goodbyes to our parents and left before breakfast en route to South Carolina. Along U.S. 82, we crossed southern Arkansas bayous, and soon Mississippi billboards pushed our hunger buttons. At a roadside eatery, the waitress brought plates of eggs, bacon, toast, and a pile of white mush with a puddle of butter in a spooned well. "What's this?" I asked.

My Arkansas accent and dialect sounded a lot like hers, and she glared in disbelief. "Why, honey, that's grits."

Explaining I had never seen or tasted grits, I turned to John. "Have you?"

He shook his head. "No. Momma was a Yankee. She never cooked them."

"Well, my mother was born and reared in Arkansas, but she never cooked grits." The waitress frowned at me, turned and walked away. Unwittingly, she made our introduction to grits a memorable marker, one recalled on many later trips across the South.

Driving into northwestern Alabama, we picked up U.S. 11 at Tuscaloosa and found a motel. The next day was Thanksgiving. We skirted Birmingham and headed for Gadsden, then into northern Georgia. Thoughts of our families' holiday tables had us salivating as we searched for an open restaurant. At last we found one and were the lone customers.

Reaching Athens, we took a southerly dip into South Carolina. Fort Jackson spread out northeast of Columbia, the capital city. We arrived in late afternoon, and John booked us into the base guesthouse, a sparsely furnished WWII barracks building.

We expected Bob and Helen Dome to arrive from Oklahoma City. I had met Helen at Fort Polk, but not him. The streetlights flickered on when they checked in at the guesthouse.

Bob, a sergeant, was an aircraft mechanic in the Oklahoma National Guard aviation unit when John joined the military group.

After greeting them, the four of us piled into Bob's Mercury convertible and went in search of a restaurant. Nestling on the backseat, John and I wished for the Bomber's comfortable heat. After dinner, we picked up an evening paper, and back at the guesthouse Helen and I circled rental ads. Since guesthouse rooms lacked any sort of entertainment in the early Fifties—television sets were rare and there wasn't even a radio—we retired early.

The next morning, John ran back into our room from the shower room. "Do you see black all over my face?" Overnight, the weather demon dropped a foot of snow, and a coal-fired furnace pumped soot through the heat vents. The room was dusted with a fine black ash. Surprised by the white ground cover and our grimy faces, we showered and hurried out to eat.

Joining the Domes in the mess hall over breakfast, we laughed about awaking with soot on our faces. Coal soot was a new experience for all of us, since we were accustomed to heat from wood and natural gas. We finished our meal and walked outside. In the wet snow, soldiers left boot-track paths leading in all directions.

With goodbye pecks on our cheeks, John and Bob wished us luck in our search for apartments. "Drive carefully," they warned as we trooped toward the Blue Bomber.

More experienced in snow than I, Helen was the designated driver. She poked at the door lock with the key, but it wouldn't slip in. After numerous tries, a passing soldier came to our aid. "You looked pretty helpless," he said, flicking a cigarette lighter and holding it near the frozen lock. It thawed in a jiff, and the Bomber rolled off the base with a slip here and a slide there.

Without access to a phone we had been unable to call ahead about rentals, but we had a city map. City streets were plowed and sanded. Soon, Helen pulled to the curb beside a large apartment building, the first address we'd circled the night before.

Leaving the car, we walked along the snow-covered sidewalk, hoping it led to the building's front entrance. Suddenly, Helen stopped to roll up her damp, flannel pajama legs. They had dropped from beneath her skirt. I didn't own long johns or other clothing suitable for such cold weather, nor was I smart enough to wear pajamas as an extra layer. We giggled about her revealed secret and the likelihood that her under-leggings would drop again.

The entrance was nowhere to be found on two sides of the building. We took a set of outside steps down to a lower level, thinking the door at the bottom might lead into the "super's" apartment.

A well-groomed young man answered our knock. We explained ourselves, and he said, "I don't know where you'll find the superintendent, but if you'll step inside, I'll point the way to the entrance." As he led us into another room, we spotted a holstered gun beneath his left arm. In the living room, another young male wore a similar weapon. The first man pointed through a window and gave directions to the front entry.

Seemingly aware of our unease, both men smiled as Helen and I edged back toward the outside door.

Hightailing back to the car, we didn't bother to find the entrance. Helen's pajama legs were down around her ankles. Apparently she didn't care as we sat in the car, gasping for breath. Finally, my older and wiser companion spoke without mentioning our stupidity. "We couldn't have afforded an apartment there anyway." She bent over and rolled up her pajamas.

"Do you suppose they're FBI?"

"Maybe," she muttered, as I looked at the next marked ad and located the address on our street map.

At this place, the last occupants left crusty, baked-on food and grease-blackened pots and skillets on the grungy gas range. I scratched off that ad, and we set out again. Over the slushy streets, we headed a few miles out to the edge of town. The next address was within easy distance of Fort Jackson, and the ad stated the new apartment complex was new and open for rentals.

An office attendant handed us a key to an apartment on the downstairs level. Letting our selves in, Helen and I stood in a large living-dining area, gaping at each other. Still agape, we walked through two bedrooms, a bath, and a well-equipped, spacious kitchen.

It was swell! "New clean!"

"Do you think we can swing the rent?" Helen asked.

My husband was a private first-class, hers, a sergeant. Giving it some thought, we looked at each other, and said, "If we share the rent."

Back at the rental office, we requested a crew to turn on the electricity. The team arrived before we left and assured us the power would be activated before we moved in the next day.

Helen and I started toward the base. We had gone about two miles when the Bomber began to fill with smoke. She pulled onto the shoulder, got out and lifted the hood. Standing beside the road, again we looked helpless, when along came the two electricians we'd just left.

They recognized us and stopped. One of them jiggled some wires under the hood. "I think you can make it to the base."

Off we went, but in minutes the car filled with smoke again. "There's a parking lot. Pull off and call John and Bob," I said.

Helen called from a public phone in the strip mall, and Bob said the two of them would be right out. They drove up in the Mercury, stepped out grinning, took one look inside the Bomber, and said, "You didn't release the emergency brake."

Breathing relief, for everything John and I owned was in the back of the car, we followed Bob and Helen back to the base. "The Bomber might need brake repairs," John said.

I sat mum, thinking any cost of repairs would be a negative when considering the big rent ahead of us.

Hesitantly, over dinner that evening, Helen and I told the guys about the "swell" apartment we rented, and how much the monthly rate was. Quickly adding, "We can afford it if we share the place."

If our husbands had any qualms, neither voiced them.

The next day, Helen and I moved into our new quarters. We shopped, cooked and ate together, and halved all the bills. Christmas came and we selected a tree from a lot, decorated it, and spread our holiday table with a traditional meal. When we had eaten our fill, we made phone connections with our cherished families back home.

The Carolina winter continued unusually cold, leaving our apartment uncomfortably chilly. Helen and I discovered heat pipes running up the inside wall of our broom closet to the second floor. Our heat was meant to radiate downward from the ceiling, but as any high school student knows, heat rises. We spent many days sitting on a shelf in the broom closet. Giggling, she said, "I have a mental image of an outdoor privy."

During the two months we lived in the Columbia apartment, the four of us whiled away most evenings polishing military boots and uniform brass to meet Leadership School regulations. During those hours, we learned all about our idiosyncrasies and each other's families.

Soon the boys conquered the two-month-long school at Fort Jackson, and it was time to move on. Parting in January, the Domes headed for Oklahoma City, and I feared we might never see our friends again, but our paths were to cross several more times in the future.

John left me in Arkansas with my family and went to Camp Polk, where he joined Bob, and they awaited orders to Army Officer Candidate School. When the orders came, they were among twenty men from the Korea-bound Forty-Fifth Infantry Division who were left behind to attend OCS.

FIRST BORN ARRIVES WHILE DADDY'S ON THE ROAD

John still waited at Camp Polk for orders to Officer Candidate School, when I woke early on an April morning with cramps. Our baby wasn't due until the first week of May, but Mother took no chances on a baby popping out into her hands. She rushed me to the Lafayette County Memorial Hospital in Lewisville. A nurse called Doctor Harrison and ushered me to a bed.

Noontime came and I showed little progress. Mother went for lunch, leaving her elderly friend in the room with me. "My phone rang all morning with news you were in the hospital. I came down here to see for myself," Mrs. Holmes said. "Push. You must push or that baby will never come." The dear old soul wanted to be helpful.

Someone entered the room and sedated me. Soon I lapsed into a near-unconscious state, but not enough for relief from frequent, swelling pains. Facing the wall, I felt a touch on my shoulder, and moaned, "John-n." Turning, I saw Doctor Harrison. "I thought you were John." My eyes pooled, and he patted my hand.

As he walked out of the room, Mother returned.

Mrs. Holmes had left without my awareness. Pains came fast and furious. Groaning and gasping through them, my mouth felt dry as a rag. I begged for water, and the doctor came with crushed ice in a cloth to wet my lips, then he hunched down in the corner of my room, waiting.

Soon, he was called out, and it was near three o'clock in the afternoon when I was wheeled into the delivery room. There stood my classmate and good friend, Nettie Lou Wells, a recently graduated RN. "Where's Thelma?" I asked about an older RN. At such a time, I wanted anyone but Nettie, with whom I had shared the better part of twelve school years.

"She went off duty at eleven this morning and I came on." She directed an aide, "Go tell Doctor Harrison she's in delivery."

In a few minutes the aide was back. "He's not in the hospital."

"Elizabeth, it looks like I might have to deliver your baby." Nettie Lou stood by with a white mask ready to plop over my nose. "Breathe in," she said.

"Oh gosh, Nettie Lou! I'm embarra—" Then, I was out like a light. When I awakened, the doctor held up my baby. "He's whole and hearty with all parts accounted for."

"A pretty boy! Lots of black hair." Nettie walked beside the aide who rolled me toward my room. "Weighs seven pounds, twelve ounces. We'll clean him up and bring him to you."

John Kilby Foster, Jr. came into the world on April 24, 1951, too late for his dad's April 20th birthday. Brother James Royal, who married us twenty months earlier, had relayed through the Red Cross to John that I was in labor. He drove the Bomber some two hundred miles from Camp Polk, but he couldn't push it fast enough to arrive before our son was born.

Around nine o'clock that night, I heard familiar voices coming from the nursery down the hall. "That's John D. Rockefeller there," my husband's father remarked. I never understood his comment, but Grandpa Foster sounded proud of his first grandchild. My heart brimmed with joy when John walked in with his parents.

I was too excited to sleep after they left. Thelma Coleman visited with me until I felt drowsy. Johnny and I were among friends who gave us doting care during the next five days.

Sometime during the hospital stay, someone filled out the birth certificate. I wanted to name our son John Carroll to pass on my birth name, but John and his mother voted down my choice. In my mind, there were reasons to reject junior, such as our child being called Johnny into adulthood.

Regardless of the tag necessary to differentiate him from his father, I knew I had the most beautiful baby in the world. Later, when an uncle said, "He looks like any other baby," I was ready to commit bodily harm.

John spent only a few days with us before returning to the Louisiana base. Baby Johnny and I were released from the hospital and returned to my parents' home. My husband drove from Camp Polk on several weekends to be with us. Then, when our baby was three weeks old, he left for six months of OCS at Fort Riley, Kansas.

Johnny was several months old when I dropped in on Nettie Lou and her mother. "Who really delivered him, Nettie, you or the doctor?" She assured me that Doctor Harrison showed up just in time.

[A scene similar to Johnny's birth might be recognized when Allise gives birth in my novel, *Southern Winds A' Changing.*]

A DIRTY DEAL ON OUR FIRST AIRPLANE RIDE

In 1950, after the second interruption of his education, John had said, "I might as well make a career of the military but not as an enlisted man." Recalled to active military service, he referred to his present rank of private first class.

Following a military man from pillar to post for the next twenty-five years had not been my idea of a happy life, but I knew I would follow him wherever his career led. Fate lays waste the best of plans, and who knows which would have been the better path? A civilian career or make the best of an Army life? Back then, we had discussed our future and agreed my husband should apply for Officer Candidate School.

In May 1951, our baby was three weeks old when his father left for Fort Riley, Kansas. I knew the next six months would be lonely, but at the same time, was relieved to have John in OCS and not in Korea with the Forty-Fifth Infantry Division.

From Fort Riley, my husband wrote of undergoing intensive studies and rigorous physical training. The Kansas River flooded, and military men were called out to sandbag against the rising water. Whether that was a welcomed diversion from day-after-day calisthenics and long marches, or not, John wrote, "Men never walk, we 'double-time' everywhere." His classes included leadership, weaponry, map reading, and other military practices.

Soon after he left, I sold our 1937 Blue Bomber to my brother and purchased a new car. Before John left for OCS, we had selected a 1951 Robin Hood green, Plymouth station wagon from a dealership in Texarkana. John's parents loaned us the money, something like $1,700.

Each month I wrote a check to them plus six percent interest, and we were debt free within a year.

Halfway through OCS, John was granted a weekend leave. He called. "Can you fly up for a visit?"

I jumped at the opportunity to see him and for him to see our child. With the date set, I made plans. Our friends, David and Ruth Gray, lived in Tulsa. I called them and explained that John could meet me there. "You're not to worry," Ruth said, "I'll be at the airport and you will stay Friday night with us. When John arrives, you can go to the hotel."

Johnny was almost four months old, and we were about to take our first airplane ride. The night before, Mother gave my teething baby a dose of something. I don't recall what she administered, but it was powerful.

Next morning, I dressed our son in a white knit suit that snapped in the crotch, brushed his dark hair and placed a white-billed cap on his tiny head. He had often been confused for a girl, so his first haircut was just before our trip. He had protested with tears and squirming, and it had taken both Mother and me to hold him still while Mr. Moore, the town barber, did the job. I was proud of our handsome little guy in his baseball cap. White socks and shoes completed his decked-out appearance.

We were ready to fly. My mother took us to the Texarkana Airport. The DC-3 sat on the tarmac, and we waved to her through the small porthole. Suddenly, the engine revved, we were rolling, the plane lifted and sailed out across a summer blue sky. Things went well to that point.

How to tell with any sense of dignity what happened next? Whether Mother's teething remedy caused the problem or not, it was a nightmare never contemplated when I thought of having babies to love and cuddle.

We were in the air about twenty minutes when I noticed dirty baby smell. Johnny needed a diaper change. Before the trip I had found disposable diapers, a new product not yet found on all store shelves, and my baby wore one. Making Johnny presentable again wasn't a concern.

Hoping the man seated next to me wasn't offended by the odor, I placed a white blanket around Johnny, unbuckled the seatbelt and with diaper bag in hand, headed for the restroom in the rear of the plane. Inside, I unwrapped my child, layer-by-layer, and peered into the worst diaper imaginable. His white suit, socks and shoes were smudged yellow. The only piece of his attire remaining unsoiled was the little white cap.

I had wiped and washed for some time, when suddenly the plane dropped. Pitching and tossing about in the small space, I held onto my baby. Why hadn't the stewardess alerted me that the plane was landing. It wouldn't have changed my situation; I was trapped in an untidy mess.

We were still on the ground when I heard a knock on the door. A feminine voice warned, "We are about to take off from Fort Smith." The third or fourth rap sounded urgent. "You *must* come out. We're ready to take off."

"I can't!" I shouted through the closed door. She surrendered, and again I rocked and rolled while clutching my child.

Soon, it was evident the smear job must end. Every paper towel in the restroom and every cloth diaper in the bag were used in the cleanup. Johnny was as clean as I could make him. Nude except for a diaper, I wrapped him in the blanket, exited the restroom, and returned to my seat.

Moments passed, then a sudden rush of nausea overcame me. I signaled for the stewardess. She offered a barf bag, and I pushed Johnny into her arms. Sitting there, struggling to spare my seat companion yet another unpleasant experience, I wondered if the young flight attendant would want a baby of her own after caring for my hastily cleansed child.

Coming to a stop at the plane dock in Tulsa, she handed Johnny to me. "He's adorable. I hope I have one as beautiful as this baby."

Stepping from the plane, I searched for Ruth. She and David married a year before my wedding, but they were childless. Ruth loved kids, yet it would be years before they had two boys and a girl. Spotting me, she came running with outstretched arms. "Let me see that boy."

A dirty diaper was still too fresh, and I shoved Johnny at her. "Here, you can keep him."

Ruth cuddled him and made baby talk as I related what had happened on our first flight. That night, she helped wash diapers, and we laughed as we told David about the dirty deal.

John flew into Tulsa the next morning, and we went to the hotel for our one night together with our baby. My husband returned to Kansas on Sunday afternoon, and Johnny and I stayed another night with the Grays.

Mother met us at the airport on Monday. I tried to give her a hard time for the awful mess on the plane, but she swore teething caused it, not her treatment.

It was November when we saw John again. He was a graduate of OCS and a commissioned second lieutenant in the Corps of Engineers. Looking physically fit, he tried to explain about the "swagger stick" officers carried. "You know, you've seen General MacArthur with one. It's a sign of authority. Officers are not to carry bags of groceries, babies or whatever."

I thought for a moment. "Sorry, Mr. Lieutenant, but you had me and this baby before you were an officer. I guess that means you will tote stuff as well as your baby."

He had a few days to get accustomed to toting our baby before we departed for Virginia.

LODGING WITH A SPOOKY MAN

In high school, I dreamed of going to William and Mary College in Virginia. The state had a romantic history, beginning with the story of Pocahontas, John Rolfe and John Smith. Magnificent photographs of the state's beauty had captivated me. Needless to say, my parents knew William and Mary was beyond their financial means. Soon any fanciful thoughts of venturing that far from home faded. But in November 1951, as luck would have it, my little family was on the road to the Old Dominion.

John was to attend the Corps of Engineer School on Fort Belvoir.

We had Thanksgiving dinner in a roadside eatery and stayed overnight in a Tennessee motel. Next morning in downtown Knoxville, we lost our highway sign. John pulled to the curb and asked a policeman, "Can you direct us to Highway 11 East?" Just then a bang was heard and the station wagon jerked forward. A woman rear-ended it. The policeman faulted her for bumping our stationary car. There was slight damage, and we got on the road again.

At the time, interstate highways were only a gleam in Presidential-hopeful Dwight Eisenhower's eye. On Route 11 East, we traveled over the Appalachian Mountains, winding around hairpin curves and enjoying the rural beauty of the Smokies and Blue Ridge ranges.

Near nightfall, we approached Washington, D. C. From the Virginia side of the Potomac River, the city bloomed under a flood of soft light. Seeing it for the first time from George Washington Boulevard (now Parkway), I thought it the most beautiful sight I had seen. I lifted seven-month-old Johnny from his canvas car seat between John and me and held him to the window. "Look! Look at the pretty lights." Oh-ing and ah-ing across the Arlington Memorial Bridge, we looked upon the Lincoln Memorial awash in light on white marble.

Driving on to the Mall, John stopped the car, and we gazed in awe at the Capitol on the hill ahead of us. Then daylight slipped away, and satisfied with the sights, we turned back to Alexandria, Virginia and booked into a motel.

After breakfast the next morning, I gathered Johnny and the diaper bag from the restaurant booth, and we set out for Fort Belvoir. Within minutes, I realized my favorite pigskin handbag was left in the restaurant. The prized watch my parents presented to me at high school graduation was in it. Back at the restaurant, the purse wasn't found in the booth, and it had not been turned in at the cashier's desk. With regret, I marked it off as a great loss.

The day didn't allow for fretting. We must find a place to live.

John drove onto Fort Belvoir, did a short tour of the base then checked in at the engineering school. Upon inquiring, he was told Bob Dome had already reported in and was given a phone number where our friend could be reached.

Helen answered the phone. They had rented a bedroom with shared bath and kitchen privileges in Lorton, a small, rural community near the fort. "The lady next door has space to rent," she said. "Come on out to our quarters."

Driving up to their abode in our Robin Hood green station wagon, we were surprised to see an identical Plymouth in a lighter shade of green parked in the driveway. Soon, we learned the station wagon belonged to the Domes. It was great to see our friends again, to share our most recent experiences, and to laugh and reminisce about living together in South Carolina.

John and Bob found reasons to laugh about their arduous OCS

training, so recently behind them. They recalled how Bob, at age twenty-seven, had pushed the age limit for OCS. How he fussed and fumed that he was "the oldest second lieutenant in the U. S. Army."

Holding Johnny, Helen appeared fascinated with our baby. It was my opportunity to thank her for being my pal in South Carolina and enduring me over those pregnant months.

Having caught up on our lives, Bob said, "Lorton is noted for the large penal facility located across the road and beyond that farmer's field." He pointed across the street. "It's about a third of a mile over there."

When our visit ended, John and I walked next door to the two-story white house with space for rent. While waiting on the stoop for an answer to the doorbell, we stared at the prison rooftop clearly visible across the field.

A thin, stern-looking elderly lady opened the door and greeted us. "Yes, I have space to rent. Come in and I'll show it to you." We followed her through the foyer, passed a staircase at the near end of the living room, and into the kitchen. She opened the door to a downward stairway, and pitch blackness obscured our view. Switching on the light, the woman led the way down the steep flight of steps.

At the bottom, we stood on the sunken level of a dirt floor. On the far side, a foot-higher, three-foot wide dirt level extended along the length and width of the large room. A wringer-type washing machine sat on the higher level beneath the only oblong window. At the back of the room an old gas range, the only kitchen appliance, rested on the same raised level. An electric cord dropped from the ceiling with a single, naked light bulb illuminating the entire space.

I stared in disbelief and started for the stairs. "No. I can't live like this, not even for a few months."

"Well, I have an extra bedroom upstairs," Mrs. Marshall said, and I stopped to listen. "My son has the other one. My bedroom is downstairs. You would share the bath with him and the kitchen with both of us. He cooks his meals." Glancing at Johnny before leading us to the second floor, she added, "My son wouldn't like a baby disturbing him."

We considered the convenience of John and Bob sharing rides to and from the fort, leaving one vehicle for Helen and me to use, and accepted the old lady's offer.

Helen and I made runs to Alexandria to shop, to the Fort Belvoir commissary for food and the Post Exchange for other everyday items. On these excursions, she shared the burden of toting Johnny.

Occasionally, we enjoyed meatloaf, veal chops or whatever-we-had dinners at the Domes' place or ours. On weekends, we visited the Smithsonian museums and other sights in the District of Columbia, as well as such historical places as Mount Vernon on the Potomac. At that time, our vehicle might be the only one parked on the Mall, a far cry from today when hoards of tourists flock to the city year round. In 1952, Washington was still a relatively small, southern town.

At nine months, Johnny pulled himself up and mouthed simple words such as "Mum" and "Dada." The stairs seemed the most daring thing he could tackle. Even though I kept eyes trained on him most every minute, one day he had to be rescued from the fifth stair step.

Mrs. Marshall let us set up his first Christmas tree in the living room. It was sheer joy to see wonder in his eyes as he gazed at the colorful lights. A Buzzer Bee pull toy was among other things he found beneath the tree.

Television sets were beyond most households' means, but our landlady had one. While Johnny napped or played on the floor, I watched the *Mike Wallace Show* and other programs.

Mrs. Marshall spent a lot of time in her bedroom located behind the dining room. She never spoke of the live-in son again after that first day. Her only infrequent visitors were another son and daughter-in-law, who lived in an almost identical, two-story white house next door. This son was a White House usher and the daughter-in-law a prison matron across the way. We learned from them that the divorced, live-in son worked at Fort Belvoir. "The only meat he will eat is liver. He's a real oddball," they said.

At night, I listened for Johnny's cries, hoping they wouldn't wake the man. We had lived there a month when we encountered him for the first time. It was on a Sunday afternoon after we returned from a sightseeing trip. When we entered the house, he sat at the kitchen table before a plate of fried liver. The man didn't speak or recognize us in any way.

John followed me upstairs, where I lay our sleeping child in his crib. Removing soiled diapers from the bag, I headed for the nappy pail kept in the basement near the washing machine. Absentmindedly, I left the door open directly behind the man and trekked downstairs.

Suddenly, the upstairs door banged with a din that raised hackles on my neck. Running back upstairs, I flung the door open and banged it shut behind me. "What the heck was that about?"

"Shut the door when you go down there. It's cold."

"You could have made your point without slamming it."

Hearing our loud voices, John came downstairs and stood in the kitchen doorway. "What's going on?" I told him, and my husband looked at the man in that steady, dependable way he has. "I will not have this," he said, and directed me upstairs.

I had committed an immature act, and the whole episode left me quite shaken. Fearing to be alone in the house with the sour-faced man, I devised an escape plan.

Helen knew about my run-in with him. If I called her for help, she was to watch our bedroom window. Should I crawl out onto the screened porch roof with my son, she was to come for Johnny and I would jump to the ground. Now, how this would have worked was anyone's guess, but my fear of the peculiar person we lived with was such that a plan comforted me, even if dangerous.

Sure enough, the time came when I thought my plan would be put to use.

On a cold afternoon, Johnny and I played on the bedroom floor when the man's old Model A Ford rattled down the long driveway. Peeping out, I saw two men in the car. I raced downstairs and rang Helen. Back upstairs, I shoved a chest of drawers against the door, picked up Johnny and rocked to keep him quiet. Listening, I waited for footsteps on the stairs.

It was my good fortune that the two men departed in the old Ford just minutes before John and Bob arrived home.

As winter settled in, the odd person was home less and less. January and February brought snow and freezing weather in northern Virginia. Laundry froze as I hung it to dry on the outdoor lines. Wash days presented another complication. Unwilling to leave Johnny alone in the house while hanging laundry, I struggled up and down the basement stairway and back steps with my baby in the stroller. Soon, John strung cord lines in the basement to solve that problem.

One day while hanging laundry outside, an excited young woman ran up to me. "I saw your car parked behind the house." She stumbled over her words. "My son is having seizures. Can you drive us to my husband's work place?"

I loaded Johnny in the car seat and sped like a demon over the rural roads. I never saw the woman again.

There were many evenings when I invited our landlady to share our dinner. She ate like a bird, and two weeks before we were to leave Virginia, she became ill. I made chicken soup, took bath water to her room, and tended her in general. After a week of this, I called her next-door son.

His wife came over. "Call her daughter in Alexandria to come for her."

I rang the daughter and was told to call a doctor. The old lady had pneumonia.

Our departure day neared and I called her son again. He gave directions to the daughter's home, and I took the sick woman to Alexandria.

At the end of February, we drove away with Bob and Helen in the lead. Back across the beautiful Blue Ridge Mountains, rounding horseshoe curves, we headed west on old Route 11.

It was as cold as a well digger's behind in Montana when we came upon a pleasant picnic site beside a rushing stream in southern Virginia. The four of us huddled around a concrete picnic table to enjoy the fare Helen and I had packed for the two-day trip. Travel meals were one way to use food that couldn't be left in a refrigerator.

We policed up our picnic leavings and back on the road, John took the lead. Both vehicles hauled all the items we owned, and our identical Plymouths, except for color, labored up the inclines. We decided our station wagons, under such conditions, couldn't pull the hat over a donkey's ears. Bob shouted from the other side of an ess curve, "Give 'em hell, John."

Toward the end of day, my husband drove through Danville and approached the Virginia-Tennessee state line when we heard a siren. In the rear view mirror, John saw the Domes speed up behind our bumper with flashing blue and red lights in hot pursuit. "Uh oh," he muttered. "Helen and Bob tried to catch up and a patrolman spotted them."

The officer pulled both station wagons over. With John and Bob's drivers' licenses in hand, he said, "Turn around and follow me back to Danville." It was ten miles back to the center of town. Arriving there, he bragged to the boys that he had caught General Mark Clark speeding. "I led him back to the courthouse, too," he said.

Our guys paid one-hundred-dollar fines, pocketed their deflated wallets, and we were underway again. Back at the state line, John pointed to a well-worn turn-around. "It's a trap. Get 'em before they get out of the state." Following his entrapment, in the future my husband maneuvered around Danville anytime our route led that way.

When we reached Little Rock the next day, the Domes headed west to Oklahoma City, and we went south to Lewisville. Shortly, we would come together again in Texas for fixed-wing flight training.

SURPRISE, YOU'RE PREGNANT!

In 1945, John had volunteered for military flight school. Flight programs closed before his desire was met, and he was discharged shortly after WWII ended. In 1948, the Army Air Corps became the U. S. Air Force, and it insisted on training all Army pilots. John had a private license in a Piper Cub J3, a small, fixed-wing plane. Now an army officer, he applied for flight training again. In March 1952, my husband received orders to the Air Force Liaison Pilot Course at San Marcos, Texas.

In the capital city of Austin, we moved into a spacious apartment on the lower level of a new ranch-style brick, the home of a retired minister and his wife. With a prestigious sounding address, 411 Riverside Drive, the house sat on a bluff overlooking the Colorado River. Considering some past living conditions, we saw it as the Garden of Eden.

A long driveway curved through well-groomed grounds shaded by huge live oak trees. The beauty and warm spring days beckoned us outdoors. I pushed Johnny in his stroller and tried to mock birds flitting among branches. Or I sat beside his playpen outside our door and called his attention to their chirping. "Listen! What's that?"

Our year-old son, who already formed a good many words, turned large brown eyes up to the sound and mimicked, "What's that?" The question became his mantra. Whenever any strange noise occurred, his eyes flared with surprise and out came, "What's that?" He didn't use his mantra the day I caught him on the kitchen floor in front of an open cabinet door with his hand in the cookie jar. His dark eyes expressed pure innocence.

We had been in Austin a couple of months, when I took Johnny on the seven-hour trip to Lewisville. It was my first extended drive without my husband. After a couple of days' visit with family, Grandma Foster returned to Austin with us. Her stay was to be short, and our landlord provided a rollaway bed for her in a vacant room next to our apartment.

Soon after Grandma left, Johnny and I rode into town and took parking meter space on Congress Avenue. I was never lucky enough to park close to my favorite department store, and in 1952, Austin didn't have parking garages. Picking up my son, I walked toward the store to buy new shoes for him.

Our purchases made, we stepped out onto the sidewalk with Johnny wearing the new mod fashion, blue and white sneakers. Sneakers replaced the leather high tops small children had worn for as long as I could remember. We walked hand-in-hand, and our little tyke toddled along until he stopped to point out his new footwear to each someone approaching.

Soon, he grew tired, and I lifted him up in my arms for the long trek back to the car. Coming up to it, my pride turned to putty. Beneath the windshield wiper was yet another parking ticket. Johnny was too heavy to tote back and forth to feed a coin-eating meter. What was I to do? Back at the apartment, I wadded and tossed it in the trash, as I had done with all the other parking tickets found on my windshield.

None of the nine destroyed tickets were ever mentioned to John. However, a time came when the Austin police mailed copies of all nine to John's senior officer. My husband paid up and warned me never to pull such a stunt again.

Parking tickets weren't a problem the day I drove out to the western edge of town, where the Colorado River widens as it ripples out of the hills. Stopping the station wagon on an incline for a traffic light, Johnny and I waited. The signal changed. I engaged the clutch and shifted the gear on the steering column. But instead of moving forward, we rolled back. People in cars behind us waited. There were no horn honks through three light changes before we got going.

It was a Sunday afternoon when John parked at the uptown-end of Congress Avenue. We walked across to the Capitol grounds, intent on touring the state building. Before reaching the entrance, we noticed a sizeable crowd gathered around a speaker. Curious, we stopped to listen to the handsome, captivating young man. Years later, we saw an evangelist by the name of Billy Graham on television and recognized the speaker heard that day in Texas.

Austin's beautiful city park, graced with huge live oak trees and a large swimming pool, lend itself to Sunday picnics. We enjoyed Sunday afternoons there with our flight school friends. When David Russell, from our hometown and then stationed at a nearby military facility, visited us, we took him there.

It was almost time for flight school to end and for us to leave Austin when I began having persistent pain in my lower back. Military doctors in Virginia had x-rayed and found two herniated disks. Since Mother's father and sister had died with tuberculosis, they suspected I had TB of the spine. "Have x-rays every six months and do not risk more pregnancies," the Virginia doctors had advised.

I went to a nearby osteopath in Austin with my ache. Imagine my surprise when he pressed on my abdomen, and said, "You're pregnant. Stop bending over at the waist to lift things. The pain comes from stressing the weak area in your spine." How he determined I was pregnant without the normal examination, I shall never know, but he was right. I was pregnant.

Clarlyn and Charlie Harris, our nearby neighbors, had no children. Clarlyn seemed thrilled when I told her I was pregnant. While our husbands were off at flight school, she fashioned on her sewing machine a brown and white checked maturity smock and a solid brown skirt for me. The skirt tied at the waist and had a round cutout for my soon-to-be bulging belly.

Charlie liked to brag, "I'm from Georgetown, the heartland of mighty Texas."

Among others in flight training with John were Bob Dome, Ralph Benefield and Jim Stevens. Jim was a native of Bryant, Texas. He and Charlie were Texas Aggies. Jim's wife, Nancy, gave birth to their first child, a girl, during flight school. Bob and Helen lived in San Marcos, and I didn't see them during the four months we lived in Austin.

Ralph Benefield amused fellow pilots with his declared method of determining wind direction. "I have a sure way to tell a wind heading. You watch for the way cows face in the fields. They turn away from wind because it tickles their noses." Needless to say, knowledge of wind direction was important to the student pilots' take offs and landings of aircraft.

As a teenager, I had lived in Houston and wasn't particularly fond of anything Texan. Leaving oodles of friends in our small town, I had one girlfriend in Houston. Jennie lived across the street and we did everything together. Daily rain showers brought steamy mist up from the heated street pavements and sidewalks. The city felt humid, winter and summer. Longing for my friends in Arkansas, I badgered my dad until he moved us back to Lewisville.

But in 1952, I found Austin a pleasant place, ranking with San Antonio as my favorite Texas towns. At that time, even though it was the home of state government and the University of Texas, the city was a relatively small place. It had the best Tex-Mex restaurant in the South. I've never found another taco encased in a potato chip-thin tortilla. The eatery was located several blocks south of the Texas Capitol and a few blocks east of Congress Avenue. Years later, we drove through Austin, looking for El Matamoras. A high-rise covered the site.

Liking a location such as Austin didn't count for anything in the military. I was learning quickly that all tours end after a few months or at the most, a couple of years. This one was about to end. John and the other guys had earned their military wings, and it was time to move on.

Our husbands had orders to Army fixed-wing flight training at Fort Sill, Oklahoma. The Air Force had taught them, now the Army would teach the way to fly. We would learn later, that such irony often occurred through inter-service policies, but our military fellows never questioned policy.

Following orders, Charlie and John left for Fort Sill in our car.

Johnny and I remained in Austin an extra day and night to do a thorough cleaning of the apartment. While defrosting the refrigerator, I removed a heavy glass cover from one of the fridge drawers and dropped it on top of my right foot. The glass broke, cutting a deep gash and raising a large knot over the long bone. Bleeding profusely, I grabbed my child, hobbled to the front door of the house, left him with the minister's wife and walked several blocks to the doctor's office. He x-rayed, found the bone wasn't broken, and applied antiseptic and bandages.

The next day, Johnny and I rode to Lawton, Oklahoma with Clarlyn.

A THUMPING BED IS A DEAD GIVEAWAY

John and and Charlie Harris left for Fort Sill in our packed station wagon. The few household items we owned had been moved so many times that given a map, they could have delivered themselves to the new Vogue Apartments on C Street in Lawton, Oklahoma.

Clarlyn, Johnny and I arrived there a day behind John and Charlie. Nancy Stevens greeted us. She was settled into the apartment next to ours on the ground floor. The Harrises moved in upstairs above the Stevens. I don't recall where the Domes rented, but it wasn't in the Vogue Apartments.

Like past, short assignments, we would be in Lawton from October through November 1952, not long enough to create many memories. On sunny fall days, I took Johnny's hand, and we strolled the sidewalk behind the apartment buildings. At one-and-a-half, he was a good age. We pointed to birds and listened to their songs, found cloud formations shaped like angels and animals. We encountered friendly dogs, among other interesting subjects. My child still stopped and asked, "What's that?"

I wasn't too keen when it came to identifying birds. Mostly, we listened and tried to mock their sounds. Sharing those walks with my small son and watching his large brown eyes fill with curiosity were the joys of my life. His first exposure to another child was the Stevens' two-month-old daughter. The baby fascinated him.

Nancy and I shared a lot of time and spoke a lot of baby blather. Clarlyn fell right into our gibberish. I already knew, and Nancy was learning, that having a child stymied intelligent conversation. We seldom got beyond discussing recipes for the evening meal and any new accomplishments of our babies.

But one day, I summoned the courage to mention the noisy newlyweds who lived above our apartment. Both worked, so our relationship was limited to speaking when we met on the stairs leading to the second floor. Their bedroom was directly over ours. Whatever their work, it couldn't have been strenuous, for their apparent energy was plentiful for the nights. On weekends and every night, their bed jitterbugged through two or three sessions. We couldn't fall into sleep soon enough to miss the thump, thumping of the bed and the blissful "oohs."

We knew right away the exercise that engaged them, but it was a while before I gained the courage to mention the upstairs activity to Nancy.

"Well," she said, "we hear it way over here in our bedroom. Clarlyn and Charlie hear it, too." The Harrises lived across the upstairs hall from the couple. We giggled happily for the young people and laughed over our husbands' expressed thoughts.

My laughter faded in a flash when John received new orders at the end of Army Fixed-Wing Training. He was ordered to Korea. Bob Dome's orders to Korea were cancelled. He went to Panama, and Helen accompanied him. Later, their two-year tour ended someplace in South America.

John was to leave in December for a year in Korea, and our second child was due in January. I called Mother and asked her to find an apartment for us in Lewisville.

KOREA LOOMED OVER THE BIRTH OF A BEAUTIFUL DAUGHTER

*L*eaving Lawton, we arrived in Lewisville in time to enjoy Thanksgiving with our parents and my brother.

Then we unpacked in one of the units of the single-storied, brick, McGee Apartment buildings. We had a living room, kitchen-dining area, bath, and one large bedroom. It was just right for twenty-month-old Johnny, our expected baby and me during the year John would be in Korea. We bought a youth bed for our son, and set it up in our bedroom along with his crib that stood ready for our second child.

John had a month-long leave time before departing for overseas. He was due to depart before Christmas, so Santa must visit early. We rushed to the Post Exchange at Barksdale Air Force Base to shop for an early Christmas.

I was desperate to bring our second baby into the world before John left for Korea.

Lafayette County Memorial Hospital sat catty-cornered from our new home. Three weeks before my due date, pains began, and John took me across the street. Doctor Harrison kept me in the hospital overnight, but it turned out to be false labor. John applied for a ten-day extension to his leave.

A week later, I went to the hospital again, and again it was false labor. This time, the doctor dismissed me, and said, "John, take her over the roughest roads you can find. Maybe that will do it." He seemed concerned for our situation.

John asked for a second ten-day extension and took me over the country roads.

Ole Saint Nick made an extra special trip with a tricycle and other toys. It was a joyous occasion for our child, even as John and I struggled with pretenses.

The third time I went to the hospital, it was the real deal. John dropped me across the street and took Johnny to his parents. He returned that morning and remained by my side until around four thirty p.m. I was rolled into the delivery room, and Doctor Harrison invited my husband in to witness the birth. As with the birth of our first child, my former classmate, Nettie Lou Wells, assisted with the delivery.

Our baby daughter, born the 23rd of December 1952 at five p.m., weighed seven pounds, eight ounces, had all her fingers and toes, a head full of dark hair and bluish eyes. I was given this information and a quick glimpse of her before she was rushed from delivery to the nursery. Back in my room in a state of drowsiness, little of the goings-on registered. I wasn't even aware of the hour when John left. The eleven p.m. hospital shift came on duty, and I heard a woman's voice from across the hall ask, "Whose blue baby is that?"

Immediately, I pushed the call button to signal a nurse. Thelma Coleman, the night nurse, walked into my room. "I heard someone inquire about a blue baby. I haven't seen my baby since she was delivered. Why not?"

"Come." She helped me from the bed, and we walked down to the nursery. "Your baby is fine. She had a problem with mucous. We cleared it and put her in the incubator." Despite her assurance, I was frightened. Our baby still had a blue-gray color, but the next morning, she appeared normal and hungry.

John approved of her name. Lindsey Ann, for my maternal grandmother's birth name, and his mother's middle name.

I returned to the apartment with our baby on the 26th. John's last leave extension ended, and the next morning, I watched him pack his bags. Rising from the bed, I went to the bathroom, and suddenly there were complications.

Doctor Harrison came to the apartment to attend me, and John's parents brought his aunt to care for the babies and me.

Johnny was twenty months, and our baby girl five-days-old. His parents took John to the Texarkana airport. There had been other separations, but this one left me with a sense of dread, fear and loneliness. Korea was a dangerous place.

Our two babies kept reality from feeling like the end of my world.

LIFE WITHOUT DADDY

I stood before the mirror in the bathroom. "Brace yourself, ole girl. You cannot fall apart today." Those words would be repeated many times during the ten months John was in Korea, and other, future separations.

The children and I settled into a daily routine in Lewisville. Things went well for the first couple of weeks. Aunt Viola provided much needed attention to Johnny, cooked our meals, cleaned and did laundry. When she left, things came unglued.

Lindsey cried nearly ever minute she wasn't nursing. On Sunday morning at First Baptist Church, the nursery attendant interrupted the service to take me to my baby. Her blanket was damp from wiping her tears. The woman said, "You can't leave her in the nursery if she is going to be crying like this." At that moment, I needed a blanket to dry my eyes.

I went to Doctor Harrison. He insisted Lindsey remain on breast milk. I wasn't producing enough, and he prescribed a formula to supplement her feedings. Over the next three months, she slept days and cried nights when not nursing. I had a real problem. Johnny was a healthy, active two-year-old with a normal sleep pattern. He occupied my days. Nights were sleepless, and the person staring from the mirror resembled "death warmed over."

Fearing suffocation of my child, I was never comfortable nursing while lying prone in bed. Night after night, I sat propped against the pillowed headboard into the wee hours, while she fed. Many times I nodded off and caught myself just before tumbling over the bedside with her in my arms.

A possibility of this happening sent me back to the doctor. Looking me straight in the eye, he said, "When *you* settle down, your baby will settle down. Your nerves are affecting her." There was no mistaking what he meant. I took him seriously, and our situation improved when she was three months old. Lindsey gained weight, cut teeth and developed a happy personality.

With her problem relieved, there was time to enjoy playing with my children, to show them photos of their daddy and to write letters to him. After Sunday church services, we alternated visits with the kids' grandparents. Mother realized I was worn to the nub, and she encouraged me to nap while she played with her grandchildren.

Every day, the babies rode with me to the post office to deliver a letter and pick up one from their father. Soon spring arrived, and we took drives along country roads. Lindsey rode in the child's car seat, and Johnny stood beside her. At the time, there was no such thing as a security belt. I shudder to think of the result had my son been thrown from the front car seat.

On our rides into the countryside, their attention was drawn to everything of interest. It could be dogwood in full bloom at the edge of the tree line, or oil well pumps in methodical motion in a field of corn stubble.

One day we rode west toward the Red River when I saw crossing the sky a long stretch of white cloud formation. In the climbing straightness of its symmetry, it was unlike any cloud formation I had ever seen. Common sense made me think it had to come from an airplane. It lay across the sky from one horizon to the other. I pointed, and Johnny and I watched in amazement for changes. A plane wasn't visible anywhere, and I must admit I felt uneasy.

We came even with Griffin's country store, and I pulled in. Just then a former schoolmate, Bobby Willis, stepped out of the store onto the porch. I pointed to the sky. "Bobby, what is that?"

"A contrail made by a jet airplane." In 1953, Bobby had already served a tour in Korea. He knew jets flew out of Barksdale Air Force Base. Jet planes were still a novelty even though they had been around since before the end of World War II. Test pilot Chuck Yeager broke the sound barrier in a jet at Edwards, California, in 1947. I read in some source that commercial airlines didn't begin using them until 1958. If that is correct, the contrail seen that day must have been made by a military jet.

Our excursions often ended at the Dairy Queen. Johnny, at three years of age, would hop down from the car and run to the window to give our ice cream orders.

While we had many such pleasant days, there were some not so pleasant. To my dismay, Johnny's one playmate was a rowdy four-year-old in the apartment building next door. He liked nothing better than to beat on my son. An only child, the mother dressed him in a cowboy suit and hat with toy pistols slung on both hips. The idea that he succeeded in intimidating my child left me more upset with his mother than with the kid. She saw what was happening and did nothing to discourage her little rascal. Not only was he rough with Johnny, but his parents didn't remove him from the chapel when he made loud noises during Sunday church services.

Protection of my child was uppermost in my mind. I wanted to ring the little bully's neck, but I only fussed with myself. However, the day came when I had enough and paid the mother a visit. "I'm sure you've noticed that my son receives the worst end of play with your child, so I've decided Johnny is too young to play with your four-year-old." Mrs. What's-Her-Name took my criticism with a smile. I told her Johnny would no longer come over to play, and asked that her child not come to our apartment.

Soon, another play opportunity presented itself. Two doors up, a nurse and wife of the hospital administrator, asked if Johnny could play with her five-year-old daughter. Thinking a girl to be gentler, I took him one morning for playtime.

It wasn't long before the neighbor brought my son home. "I caught my daughter playing doctor with Johnny." The young girl tried to take his rectal temperature with a fountain pen.

The only other neighborhood child belonged to Albert and Loretta Plafcan, across from us in the other apartment building. Their first child, a daughter, was a month older than Lindsey. She and Marilyn learned to walk about the same time.

Johnny was left without a playmate until our across-the-street, elderly neighbor, Mrs. Wilbanks, called to ask if he and Lindsey could play with the children she babysat. I don't know what I would have done without this kind lady who called often when she kept Helen Powell's kids. Mrs. Wilbanks babysat for me, too, when I had the need.

I was grateful to have my children. They filled time. Friends were scarce. Only one classmate, Nettie Lou, the nurse, was still in town. High school graduates usually went away to college or moved to jobs locations. Lewisville presented few opportunities for young people.

There were older friends but they, like Nettie and Wilma Wilbanks, held jobs and were only free on weekends.

I recall leaving the children with Mother a few times to see a movie. At night I was home with my babies. I came to cherish nighttimes after the kids were put to bed, claiming the time as my own. John had gifted me with a Pfaff sewing machine the Christmas before he left for Korea. While my sewing experience amounted to fashioning a bibbed apron and a simple blouse for a high school Home Economics class, I braved a new pastime. On many nights my light burned until two o'clock in the morning, while I sat at the machine.

On one of those late nights, the doorbell rang. Without a thought to danger, I left the sewing and opened the door. From the outside darkness came a male voice. "Is this the hospital?"

"No, it's across the street. See the lights?" I pointed.

"Oh," he said, turning and walking away as I closed and re-locked the door.

Later, on the way to the bedroom, I glanced out the kitchen window. The Plafcan's kitchen lights were on, and I stood watching Albert and the man who had just left me. Soon, they moved back to the Plafcan's front door. Dismissing what I had seen, I showered, got into bed but hadn't gone to sleep when I heard garbage cans clanging about behind our building. Dogs, I thought.

The next morning at the post office, someone said, "A man tried to obtain drugs from the hospital late last night. The sheriff was called, but he escaped across your backyard."

There was another night when Lindsey had difficulty breathing. Nettie Lou answered the hospital phone. To my frightened voice, she responded, "Put a pot of water on the stove, bring it to a boil and hold her above the steam with a towel over your heads." Laughing, she assured me Lindsey would soon breathe well. I followed her instructions, returned my baby to the crib and lay listening to her gasp for air. The sound was beyond endurance, and I called Nettie again.

"Bring her over."

"I can't. Johnny's asleep. I can't leave him."

"Yes you can. I'll meet you at the hospital door. It will take only a minute."

At the hospital, I handed over my child. "Come for her in the morning," Nettie said.

Early the next morning, I found Nettie Lou laughing and playing with Lindsey. She bragged about the fun they had.

Sometime during the year, Grandma Foster wrote to John that I never came out to visit them. The children and I visited every other Sunday after church. She wrote that when they stopped by my house, I wasn't home, complaining that I was always at my parents' home. Mother did have us out for dinner often. She knew I had little incentive to cook for myself. I would drive out, eat dinner and be home with the kids by seven o'clock, their going-to-bed time.

I even went several times a week to John's parents to buy eggs and milk from Grandma. Often I took John's letters for them to read, since he didn't write to them every day.

Grandma's letter prompted my husband to write me about his mother's complaint. Upset, I kept John's letter handy. When Grandma and Grandpa stopped by, I read it to them. "Do you think it was wise to write this when he's faraway and there's a possibly of his plane being shot down?" I asked. John flew reconnaissance missions over Korea.

"Well, that's the way I see it," Grandma said. We had a few words in which I told her how it was going to be with me. If allowed, she could be domineering. I decided she would not intimidate me. I think Grandma Foster appreciated that I stood up for myself. We never had another cross word. Yet, when I asked for the oak dining room furniture John inherited from his grandfather who died just before we married, Grandma said we could move it when John came home. I think she wanted to be sure the furniture stayed in the family line in the event something happened to John. She was funny that way.

The year 1953 was winding down. John wrote he would be home from Korea two months early. A rule required U. S. soldiers to be on the front line for six months before moving back for six months. Somehow my husband was overlooked and remained up front for ten months.

In November, Johnny, Lindsey and I went to meet him at the Texarkana airport. Happy days again! His son ran to his father, shouting, "Daddy!" Lindsey fell right into his arms. It was as though they had been with him over the last ten months rather than looking at photos.

Christmas came, and one night we took the kids to First Baptist Church for Santa's visit. One-year-old Lindsey totted down the aisle to see him. Curiosity satisfied, she returned to us.

We picked up life where it left off almost a year earlier, and when new orders came, we packed up for the move to Fort Hood, Texas.

BUY ANOTHER DIAPER PAIL

In early January 1954, we left Lewisville and headed for Fort Hood, Texas. John had purchased a used, four-wheel trailer to haul our material possessions—a youth bed, baby crib, breakfast table with four chairs, pots, and pans. In all, it wasn't much. With the loaded trailer hitched behind the station wagon, we had gone as far as the west side of Texarkana, a distance of about twenty-five miles, when the conveyance collapsed.

What was it about this town that delayed us each time we traveled through it? Memories of the Bomber's flat tire and headlight failure made me think we should circumvent Texarkana.

John called his dad, who came to our rescue with his boat trailer. Reloading and strapping down our goods, we headed out again, leaving the broken trailer in Grandpa's hands.

Fort Hood, slightly west of what is now Interstate 35, covered a huge area west of Waco and Temple. Established as Camp Hood in 1942 for WWII training purposes, when the war ended, the post population dropped to less than two thousand. In 1950, with outbreak of the Korean War, the temporary camp was given permanent status as a fort. By 1954, it was the nation's only military installation housing two divisions—First and Fourth Armored, as well as Third Army Corps Headquarters. Around that time, rural towns near the base, including Killeen, began to grow.

[As this is written, Fort Hood is one of the world's largest military installations, and Killeen is a densely populated area, having moved from an agrarian to cosmopolitan environment.]

Arriving there, we gave up our quarters' allowance for a two-bedroom duplex apartment in the Wherry Housing Project just outside the base gate. This was to be John's first two-year assignment. Time to buy furniture. We shopped in Killeen, which edged on the south border of the base. Newly constructed mercantile buildings lined the town's unpaved main street. Extending the length of the buildings, a sidewalk rose about two feet above the street.

We purchased living room seating, tables and lamps, and a bedroom suite then stepped out on the sidewalk. An army of crickets—Jimminy Cricket-size—hopped on the paved walk and clung to storefront windows. One-year-old Lindsey toddled along, picking them up and giggling when they tickled her hands.

Soon our new furniture was delivered, and we settled into the Wherry community at 115 Graves Drive. Built to house the military, all the duplexes stood one-story high and wore dark green paint. Grass green lawns were treeless, and we wouldn't know until summer that arid Texas earth dried and cracked open.

Johnny and Lindsey, our two Army brats, soon made friends with children on our side of the street. Through them, we became acquainted with other parents.

At the top of Graves Drive, the Army chaplain and his wife had a six-year-old daughter. Next door to them, Johnny found a playmate with a de-scented, pet skunk. His new friend moved away shortly after we settled in, a first lesson for our son that playmates frequently moved.

On down our side of Graves Drive, a Jewish couple and their two small girls lived in the duplex building with the street bully and his parents. Older by a couple of years, the young boy beat up every male younger than he.

I don't recall that anyone lived in the other side of our duplex when we moved in. Later, a family of Seventh Day Adventists occupied it. The father was a doctor with wife and two or three older girls. I shall never forget the doctor's remedy for my chronic sore throat. Over the years, it served our entire family, and still does. Wet a towel with cold water, wrap it around the throat then wrap a dry towel around the wet one. Remarkably, the fever is drawn out and discomfort is relieved.

We had never known anyone of that sect, but soon learned Adventists worshiped on Saturdays, drank a lot of Ovaltine, observed dietary restrictions, and were lovely neighbors.

The duplex below us was home to Major Johnny and Marianne Spencer. A few years older than John and I, the Spencers had no children. Marianne, a beautiful redhead, was from Australia. Her husband was a native of Stamps, Arkansas, a town four miles east of Lewisville.

In the same duplex with the Spencers, Captain Snow, another doctor, lived with his wife and two blond-haired boys the ages of Johnny and Lindsey. Several other duplexes stood between them and the end of the street. One housed a couple with one small son Lindsey's age. The child had a crop of beautiful brown curly hair. At the end of our street, Captain Fred Weller and his wife, Dorothy, occupied the last apartment with a couple of sons older than our kids. Fred was assistant operations officer in the First Aviation Company to which John was assigned. He left military service a year or so after we came to Fort Hood, and we heard that both he and Dorothy attended law school, and rose to judgeships in Texas.

Looking back, I find it odd that we didn't know people on the other side of the street.

About a month after we settled in this new place, I learned I was pregnant for the third time. Soon, new friends laughed and said, "Yeah, you have to be careful of the water you drink." One said, "Maybe you swallowed a watermelon seed."

After two pregnancies, I knew it wasn't water or a melon seed. Counting back on the calendar, it resulted from the first time John hung his pants on the bedpost after coming home from Korea.

I can't say I was happy about the situation. Hot weather approached, and the prospects of a new baby added to the responsibilities of caring for a four-year-old and one almost two. Oh well, buy a new diaper pail, I thought with resignation, and reminded myself that our children may make work, but they provided many memorable happenings.

Just let them out of sight for a few moments, and you were in for big surprises. Such as the day Lindsey, a most precocious child, found my lipstick and did a make-up job on her self and the little boy with curls.

His mother took him home for a cleanup, but the next time they visited, there wasn't much she could do to remedy what happened. Lindsey completed her beauty treatment with a pair of children's scissors. She was caught holding the scissors and most of the kid's brown curls lay all over the back steps. His remaining hair was badly gapped. This ended our relationship with the mother, and soon the family had orders to move.

At Easter time, we drove out into the countryside, looking for a place to hide eggs. We came upon a large patch of Texas Blue Bonnets. With Johnny and Lindsey supposedly covering their eyes in the car, John hid the eggs. Johnny filled his basket, but Lindsey was more interested in sitting among the blue bonnets and plucking them apart as if to say, "He loves me, he loves me not."

When we were ready to head home, she wouldn't get in the car. We coaxed to no avail, and finally, "We're leaving without you, Lindsey."

From the back seat, Johnny said, "I don't want you to leave my sister." He called to her, and soon Lindsey came to the car.

With the collection of children on our street, each birthday celebration brought the same kids to every party, and these parties were frequent. I don't recall many social activities at Fort Hood. We bathed and dressed our two in their pajamas and went to the drive-in movies. They were asleep before the double feature ended.

On the night of July 31, we saw two movies and arrived home late. With the kids tucked in, I took a shower and crawled into bed. In a few minutes, my scream brought John from the bathroom with a towel in hand. He was wet from the shower, I was wet, the bed was wet. My water had broken two weeks before the due date.

I had a history of early deliveries. Johnny and Lindsey were born two to three weeks earlier than the doctor's predicted time, and now another baby was just as eager to enter the world.

Marianne had offered to stay with the children, day or night, when it came time for me to go to the hospital. Despite the late hour, John called, and she came right over in nightgown and robe. John drove to the base hospital, dropped me off and returned home to relieve her.

I walked into the delivery section of the WWII-structured building and was told to get on a gurney. Someone rolled me to a place outside the cluster of four delivery rooms, all of which were occupied, and parked my wagon near the nurse's station.

The hour was around 2:30 in the morning, and it seemed moments stopped and held in a grip of pain. A nurse checked me at timed intervals, and on each occasion, I repeated, "Don't give me a spinal. My osteopath said with my back condition, it wasn't advisable."

After what seemed too long a time and too much pain, someone wheeled me into a delivery room. On a last gasp before the birth, a nurse slapped a mask with anesthetic over my face. Steven Carroll Foster was born August 1, 1954 at six a.m. He weighed seven pounds, two ounces.

I was rolled down to the new mothers' ward, a large room, long and wide with lots of windows. At feeding times, babies came into the room on a train of three or four long connected carts. They lay head to head, lining both sides of the carts, and each mother left her bed to retrieve her newborn.

Sometime during our hospital stay, I was told Steven was the one-thousandth baby born in the Fort Hood hospital. I failed to ask if one-thousandth that year or for all time.

Several days after we brought Steven home, a wrack of pain, similar to labor, besieged me. Captain Snow came over. "It will pass," he said. "This happens sometimes after giving birth."

Our baby was two weeks old when Dewey Crank drove Grandpa Foster's car, bringing both grandparents, his wife, Imogene, and son Gayther to see the grandparents' second grandson. They brought three or four of Grandpa's red and yellow-centered watermelons. We chilled them and had a feast on the lawn. Our visitors slept in a motel during their visit.

When they returned to Arkansas, our attention focused on our growing family's need for more beds. Steven inherited the crib, and we purchased bunk beds for Johnny and Lindsey.

A new baby required attention, limiting that given to our other two. One day Lindsey, lacking a few months being two years old, went missing. I walked up and down the sidewalk behind the duplexes, calling.

Across the street, I described what she was wearing. "Have you seen my little girl?"

No one had seen her.

Ready to phone the police, I saw a young girl coming across the wide grassy area separating the backs of our buildings. She held my daughter's hand. Laughing, she said, "I found her in our yard and took her inside to play."

Relieved and happy to see my little scamp, I laughed, too.

"Baby boom"-producing mothers didn't work outside the home. It was a time before families needed a second car. However, it soon became evident that I needed the car to make hospital runs for ear infections or sniffles, and to shop at the Base Exchange and commissary. We lived a short distance from the main gate of the post, and the aviation company was just inside the entrance. John bought a Cushman Motor Scooter to commute to and from work.

Johnny, now four years old, listened for the scooter to turn onto our street then ran to meet his dad for a ride.

We were in Texas almost a year when the Adventist family moved, and a young couple with a baby daughter took their apartment. The husband was a military policeman, and his wife, Marilyn, a native Texan. Our babies were about the same age, and Marilyn and I shared babysitting when errands were run. We shared recipes, too.

Her beef marinade called for one fourth cup of lime juice, two or three minced garlic cloves, and one half cup of olive oil. Marinate two steaks overnight and grill.

Her Dumpling Pie recipe: Heat oven to 375 degrees. Melt one stick of butter or margarine in a 9x9-inch baking dish. Mix ½ cup of flour, ½ cup of sugar, 1 teaspoon of baking powder, then stir in ½ cup of milk. Pour mixture over the melted butter. Spoon two cups of fresh or a can of well-drained fruit, such as apples, peaches, pineapple, berries, cherries, or strawberries over the batter. Bake 30-40 minutes or until tested done with a toothpick.

Some fruits required sugar or sweetener. A dollop of ice cream complimented the dessert. I used her quick and delicious dessert recipe many times, and still do.

Like his siblings before him, Steven nursed four times a day. Marianne, my Australian friend, knew I sat down in the rocking chair with the baby around 10:00 each morning. Every day but weekends, I could count on her to visit until noon. While I enjoyed my entertaining friend's company, I watched the dust bunnies gather beneath furniture.

Our baby soon learned to sit on his own, and when John rode his Cushman home for lunch, we sat on the floor playing pat-a-cake and other baby games with him. His giggles thrilled us and he was a joy to watch.

Soon Steve was a year old, and as Johnny and Lindsey had, he walked early. He toddled about well by the time Mother, Dad and Frank visited. One afternoon, Dad shed his shoes and napped on our bed. Steven slipped in and tried out his new teeth on Grandpa Carroll.

Letting out a loud yelp, Dad came in laughing and showing his foot. "That little scamp bit my big toe!"

When time came to cook evening meals, I put Steven in the stroller and parked it in the kitchen. Three babies had cut teeth on the wooden beads and smeared food on the blue canvas material. The conveyance was getting rather threadbare.

Our second summer in West Texas, dry soil cracked in the worn path beneath the clothesline. Days were too hot for strolling a baby. The arid climate required a "swamp cooler." An attached water hose dampened a filter in the large window unit, which pulled cooled air into the house. For more than four years, I had washed and hung diapers outdoors to dry. Unlike Virginia's freezing weather, at Fort Hood, I didn't have to worry about clothes drying.

It didn't rain often, but it must have at least once. Or was it the lawn sprinkler that made the puddle where Steve played? Dressed in nothing but a diaper, he splashed himself into a happy, muddy mess.

A psychiatrist might uncover a few hang-ups from my kids' early potty training.

Twenty months was the time span between Johnny and Lindsey, and nineteen between her and Steven. Heaven knows, I had to train them early, for babies were bumping into other babies. We had gone through two diaper pails and the washing machine splished and splashed in a steady workout.

Weather was predictable at Fort Hood, and military maneuvers were common occurrences. One had just ended when I answered the phone and some man had a message for Marianne. He was unable to get her on the phone and asked that I relay the message that her husband was delayed. I rang her several times without a response. She didn't drive and was always home when her Johnny was away.

Concerned, I walked over and knocked on the front door. When she didn't answer, I turned the knob, eased the door slightly ajar and called upstairs. Then, a glimpse caught bodies rolling from the couch to the floor. Johnny was home! One didn't have to guess what was going on. Embarrassed, I banged the door shut and ran home. Later,

Marianne came over, and laughing, she said Johnny wanted me to know, "there was a lot of man left."

Turned out there was enough of my own man. Steven was only a few months old when we drove to our hometown for our family doctor to perform a vasectomy. We couldn't be sure John was "fixed" until Steven was weaned.

Sometime in 1955, my husband went to Fort Sill, Oklahoma, for two months of helicopter school. And sometime between his temporary duty assignments, I became impregnated again. John wasn't fixed! And our prescribed birth control method hadn't worked.

I was just a Fertile Myrtle and John was always ready to plant.

We returned to Lewisville, and the doctor tried the surgery a second time. He said John had two sets of what's-it. I wanted to tell Marianne's husband that he wasn't half the man my husband was, but embarrassment and upset about the unplanned situation kept me from it.

After Johnny was born, each time I shared an expected baby with Mother, her response was always the same. "Oh no!" She knew how to put a little dark cloud over that news. Nevertheless, she came to help after the births, adored each child that came along, and she wasn't the reason for the vasectomy. A military doctor x-rayed my herniated spine every six months and advised against having more children.

Well there I was, pregnant for a fourth time. I was six or seven months along when John said he had a week of TDY to attend a conference in Southern Pines, North Carolina. I was too tired to rest. "I'm going with you. We'll leave the three kids with their grandparents. I've never asked them to keep our children. Surely they can give me a week of much needed time off."

I called and received a weak "yes," but I didn't question it.

I had never left my children except to go to a hospital, and was close to tears for most of the drive to North Carolina. John booked into an inn with a long front porch and rocking chairs lining the length of it. While he and several other guys from Fort Hood attended daily meetings, I stayed in the room, reading or working crossword puzzles.

Occasionally, I rocked on the porch and watched the street traffic. In the evening, I had dinner with John and our friends.

One evening, we played Bingo on the lawn of some place that drew a large crowd. During one round I told John I had a bingo, "but I'm not about to waddle up there in front of all these people in my condition."

"Bingo!" John yelled. The emcee checked the numbers, and it wasn't a bingo. Wrapped in embarrassment, my husband looked as though he wanted to sink into obscurity.

Back in Killeen and three weeks before Thanksgiving, the Blue Bolt maneuvers began in Louisiana. The battle exercises involved four divisions—including John's aviation company— over a six-week period, ending in mid December.

While John was away, I shopped for Christmas. I waited in a line to pay for purchases when I discovered my wallet was missing. A clerk helped me search down the counters I had frequented, but we didn't turn up the billfold.

Devastated, I wrote a check for the purchased items and drove home. I called the police. The next day, they called me. They found my wallet on the street next to the curb with my military ID card and driver's license still inside. John called from Louisiana, and I wailed into the phone. "Eighty dollars were stolen when someone lifted my wallet." I assumed the thief took it from the purse hanging on my shoulder as I pushed through a crowded doorway into the department store.

I was about eight weeks from delivering our fourth child when John left for Louisiana. Facing another holiday without him, I called Mother. "If you will take a bus to Killeen and celebrate Thanksgiving with us, I will take you back home." Dad was out of town, and she agreed to visit.

Arriving a few days later, she sat in our living room with Marianne and me when we heard a rap on the back door. A friend returned to the base from the maneuvers and dropped in to tell Marianne and me that our husbands were faring well. On the way out the door, he turned and said, "Maneuver training will shut down for Thanksgiving Day, but the men can't come home."

Marianne said she would like to be with Johnny for the holiday.

"Well," our acquaintance said, "I can tell you how to call him over the field telephones." He gave us the number for reaching Grizzly, the division headquarters. "When Grizzly answers, say 'give me Able.' When you get Able, ask for Baker, then for Charlie."

As Marianne and I mulled over his information, I realized the relief I expected from Mother's visit did not fill the lonely void left by John's absence. She had kindly answered my call, but a less-than-enthusiastic holiday mood persisted. Dreary weather darkened the sky and threatened to dump rain anytime. It added to the mood.

The more Marianne and I talked, the more I knew she felt as I did. It just seemed reasonable to take some kind of action. If we headed for Louisiana, dropped off Marianne to join her Johnny, then Mother, the kids and I would go on to Lewisville for Thanksgiving. My poor mom. I don't know what she thought, but she did the wise thing and never objected.

We packed quickly and with everyone in our 1954 Dodge sedan, we hit the road.

Heading east, we hadn't gone far before heavy sheets of rain pelted down. The farther we went, the harder it stormed. For miles and miles, we were the only vehicle moving in our direction, but a steady stream of headlights came at us. Creeping along at a snail's pace of ten to twenty miles an hour, in and out of heavy squalls, the electric windshield wipers made no more than thirty swishes per minute. Our gray sedan hadn't seen much wet weather in West Texas, so the slow windshield action was a surprise.

Johnny sat on the front seat between Marianne and me, his eyes staring through the windshield at the road ahead. "Mom, I'm helping you drive." We skipped from one lighted service station canopy to the next, pulling beneath and waiting for the torrent to slacken. Almost as soon as we reentered the highway, another gale began.

Following the white line at the shoulder's edge, I distinguished no more than a few feet ahead. After four hours on the road in heavy rain, we arrived in Leesville, Louisiana. November's early darkness crept into the daylight. We stopped at a station to refuel the car and to let Marianne call her Johnny. On the station's public phone, she dialed the Grizzly number. Back in the car, she told how easy it was to reach him using the military-in-field system. Her husband told her to remain at the station and he would send someone for her.

While the attendant filled the gas tank, I went to the phone and dialed. A male voice answered, "Grizzly."

Then I said, "Give me Able, please." Able answered. "Baker, please." Next, "Charlie, please."

Finally a voice said he would get Lieutenant Foster right away.

Soon John's familiar voice came over the wire. "Where in God's name are you? I'm out here in the rain, answering a phone hanging from a pine limb."

Feeling meek, I answered, "We're in Leesville."

"What *are* you doing?" My explanation that Mother was along, and we were on the way to Lewisville for Thanksgiving did not make my husband happy. After all, the doctor said I was six weeks from delivering our fourth baby. I told John we were leaving Marianne at the station, and Johnny was sending someone for her. Then we were going on to Lewisville. We hung up with that understanding.

Back at the car, the attendant asked where I was headed. "Shreveport, then Arkansas."

Shaking his head and pointing, he warned, "You better stay off this highway. Tanks have run up and down it. Chewed the shoulders down two feet. It's raining and already dark."

"How should I travel?"

He directed me on a route northeast through the town of Alexandria. I took out a road atlas and planned the way. The circuitous road took us to Jonesboro, the town near where Marianne's husband was encamped. She got back into the car, and we headed that way.

The farther we traveled, the less rain we encountered. Around 2:30

a.m. we arrived in Jonesboro and stopped at another service station. Marianne went inside to make another call.

Soon she returned to tell us that even in the early morning hour, she had reached someone who was to let her Johnny know where she would be

Just then, a young GI stepped up to the car window. "I was trying to sleep on my duffle bag in the station when I heard her," indicating Marianne, "mention Lieutenant Foster. I know him, and I can take you right out to him."

I don't know what I was thinking, and Heaven only knows what Mother thought, but Marianne unloaded her bag and walked back into the station.

The GI took the wheel of our car. Looking back on the event, I can guess that he was due back with his unit before roll call, and we were his way of avoiding an absent-without-leave (AWOL) charge.

He took us over several miles of muddy cow paths to a flat open space surrounded by dense woods. Johnny was awake, but Lindsey and Steven slept on the back seat with Mother who never uttered a peep. Parking in what appeared to be a deserted meadow, the soldier left the car to go for John.

Off in the distance, hoot owls broke the eerie silence of an eerie, pitch black, rainy night.

Some time passed when a figure materialized from the tree line. John walked to the car window and pushed back his poncho. "What in God's name are you doing out here?" Again, he listened to my explanation. Then, "You go back to that station. I'll come in the morning and drive you to Lewisville." He vanished back into the dark forest.

I returned to the station, hoping to catch a few winks of sleep. After several hours, a two-and-a-half ton, flatbed truck, loaded with GIs, pulled up beside the car. John jumped down from the truck.

Major Melvin Fields, his First Combat Aviation Company commander, had refused permission to drive us to Arkansas. and had added John's name to his "little black book." Oops, learning to transition from free spirit to live by rigid military rules sank into my head slowly.

John must have considered getting me to a safe destination before I had the baby. At any rate, he used his clout as the First Armored general's pilot and went over his company commander's head. He explained our predicament to our friend, Colonel Jack Blohm, the division aviation officer. The colonel, well known among his officers for taking care of his men, knew I was ready to deliver a baby. He found a legitimate way for John to drive us to Lewisville.

We arrived at my parents' home around mid-morning. That afternoon, an aviation company fixed-wing plane flew into the town's airport, picked up John and dropped him and repair parts for a downed helicopter. With some minor problem, the pilot had landed the chopper near Ruston, Louisiana. John flew the repaired craft back to the maneuver-landing site.

While this took place, Mother cooked Thanksgiving dinner, and several days later, the kids and I returned to Fort Hood.

Although black listed in Major Fields' book, John never received punishment for my caper, but I got a lot of teasing from the officer. From my husband's comments, I got the impression he believed my foolishness was a deliberate attempt to visit him, and had nothing to do with the dangerous road damaged by tank traffic. Had I known he was near Jonesboro that might have been the case.

At the end of the Blue Bolt maneuvers in December, John returned home with news that the entire First Armored Division was ordered to Camp Polk, Louisiana. Before Fort Hood, we had lived in one place no more than a few months. Now, the first two-year assignment was ending. It was time to move again.

SEARCH FOR A HOSPITAL BED
AND PILLOW

After two years in the duplex apartment, I looked forward to new quarters. Unlike some military wives who dreaded the preparations a move required, or regretted pulling up roots frequently, I looked forward to a fresh, clean house. Two weeks before Christmas and a month before the anticipated delivery of our fourth child, our household belongings were packed and loaded on a cross-country moving van, ready to head for Leesville, Louisiana.

Camp Polk had been closed twice and was about to be opened for the third time. Built in 1941, it closed at the end of World War II and reopened in 1950 at the outbreak of the Korean War. My introduction to the post was then, when John was there with the Forty Fifth Infantry Division. It closed again when the Korean conflict ended. Now, it was to be reopened for a third time as a permanent post, and renamed Fort Polk.

At the end of the Blue Bolt maneuvers in Louisiana, the First Armored officers were told the division was moving to Fort Polk. On receiving this news, Colonel Blohm called his aviation officers together. "We're flying to Leesville to find housing for our families," he said. The men in John's unit rented every available house in a 1950s development. Needless to say, the general's staff and other division officers were ticked-off about the jump on housing.

So, with enough clothing packed to last three days, in case our moving van didn't arrive within a reasonable time, we watched the loaded van pull away from the curb. Then, we hit the high road to Louisiana along the same route Mother, the kids, Marianne and I had recently traveled.

Our trip halted a few miles west of Leesville at a huge motel sign reading, "101 Units." Leesville was a small town, and we couldn't be sure of finding overnight lodging. John pulled in front of the office, and we saw familiar cars in the parking lot. Some of our Fort Hood friends had arrived ahead of us.

After five years as a military wife, I thought I could no longer be surprised, but there aren't words to describe our motel unit. Consisting of two rooms, one housed an old gas cook range and a bed. The range leaked. We called the desk. Someone came, checked the leak, and reported he would call a plumber but repair would be the next day.

It was mid-December. We requested more blankets and opened all the windows. John and I took the gas-scented room. The thin mattress on our bed sloped to the center, leaving us to roll together in a welded position. Turning over meant riding a wave of bedsprings. Bed tides, mattress slopes and noxious odor did nothing to promote sleep. I lay awake, thinking my kids might possibly be sacrificed to asphyxiation.

The toilet was another story. A walk through the kids' bedroom led to a flight of outdoor steps and down to a small, detached room. If one expected to bathe, no such place was provided. John and I had bedded down in some low-class places, but this one took the prize.

Next morning, we breathed relief. All of us had survived "101 Units."

I was ready to face whatever our new address at 2104 Jean Street presented. We had just left dark green siding in Killeen's Wherry housing. Now, all the houses in the development wore dark green siding and had attached garages.

Familiar faces of Fort Hood friends offered a beam of joy we could latch onto.

Early in John's military career, his tours of duty were set to end just before Christmas. It was never a convenient time to move, but here we were. I listened to other wives complain of having to shop for Christmas.

Fortunately, with a baby ready to come out of the oven, I had completed most of my holiday shopping before we left Texas. We unpacked toys and stashed them in the garage, a safe place, we thought. Apparently, five-year-old Johnny peeked. One day I looked out the window and saw him riding down the driveway on his sidewalk scooter. Thinking quickly, I told him it was his gift from grandparents, and they would be disappointed if they knew he didn't find the scooter beneath the tree.

If Santa visited Leesville stores that year, we missed him. Getting settled in the new house and celebrating Lindsey's third birthday was enough to leave this pregnant woman pooped. We put up a tree, decorated it, and Santa Claus came. Three days later, and two weeks after leaving Fort Hood, I called John. "Can you come home and see after our kids?"

Apparently, he saw I had used my last ounce of energy. "I'm taking you to the hospital."

"No, please. Just see to the kids. The hospital isn't ready for patients. Anyway, I saw the doctor yesterday, and he said I would deliver the baby in January."

My husband insisted. Like my mother, I suspected he didn't want to take a chance of having a baby drop in his hands. He took me to the hospital and returned home with the children.

Preparations to receive patients in the WWII building hadn't even begun. The only person on the premises was a nurse. She rushed about, calling the only doctor and searching for a bed, pillow and place to stash me. At nine o'clock that night, 28th of December 1955, with a corpsman attending, the doctor held up my newborn. "It's a boy," he said.

"It can't be!" I looked at my infant in disbelief.

So much for old wives' tales. "If it's a girl, the baby is carried high." Or was it low?

Convinced our unborn child would be another girl, I had given no thought to a boy's name. Settling on Mary, in honor of John's mother, I pulled Kay out of the hat for no reason at all. Mary Kay.

Whew. Imagine a kid going through life with the same name as a cosmetic and skin care products distributor.

I was still on the delivery table when the doctor filled out the birth certificate. He asked for my baby's name. I pulled David out of the blue and turned to him. "What is your name?" He answered Raymond Nielsen. Tact fell by the wayside. "I don't like Raymond, but how do you spell your middle name?" The Nordic spelling appealed to me, but it was misspelled Nielson on the birth certificate.

David Nielson Foster weighed six pounds, twelve ounces. As the only patients, my newborn and I received lots of attention. Although Mother arrived before we were released from the hospital, John was the only visitor allowed to see us. He brought Mother and the children to a spot behind the building and opposite my window. I waved to them.

Bringing our new baby home meant beginning a new cycle of diaper laundering. Each load in the washer and dryer started the machines in a dance across the kitchen floor. Mother placed Johnny, Lindsey, and Steven on top of the appliances, hoping the added weight would hold the machines in place. The kids giggled, but their fun ended when we had the machines leveled.

Mom stayed a week. When she left, I hired a full-time African American for two dollars per day. Each morning, I picked her up in "colored town" and returned her around four p.m.

Our new baby faired no better than Lindsey had on breast milk. He was six-weeks-old when the doctor recommended pasteurized milk. Soon, he grew plump and as happy as a clam.

Considering that I wanted to jump from the highest building in Texas when I learned I was pregnant for a fourth time, and considering his miraculous conception, our David was, and still is, a blessing to all our family. A few years ago, I told him how he happened to be conceived after his father's vasectomy. We had a good laugh.

With daytime help and a happy baby, there was time to enjoy our neighborhood friends and participate in military wives' activities. Colonel Blohm's wife called a meeting of the Aviation wives in her home and apprised us of a Louisiana law on the books since emancipation. "Ladies," she said, "we have a black lieutenant with a black wife in the unit. I must inform you that it's against the law in Louisiana to entertain Negroes in a white home. Don't do it. This couple will join us any time on the base, but socializing with them off-base is prohibited."

I don't know how others felt about such an outrageous law, but it disturbed me.

Later, I met the handsome couple at some on-base affair and was captivated by their sophistication and congeniality. I don't recall seeing them often. It's quite possible the lieutenant wasn't with the unit long, but I've often wondered about them.

Under the impression that Fort Polk would be a two-year tour, we purchased a house in DeRidder. David was four months old when we moved twenty-six miles away from the post and our Leesville friends. Our new address at 30 Country Club Circle put us in a development built around a small lake. Thirty tall pine trees surrounded our three-bedroom brick home. Soon, a chain-link fence was installed around the back yard to keep our small ones corralled.

Jack and Penny Kleuver and their youngsters, a military family from Fort Hood, lived two doors away. Our immediate neighbors were the Gordon Foremans and their new baby.

Soon I found another African American to work full-time. Eddie was almost as round as she was tall. She provided superb help, even moving heavy furniture to clean, and taking excellent care of our children. She was there when John was hospitalized for four or five days at Fort Polk with a bad case of poison ivy. Her broad smile could light up a Christmas tree. My husband came in contact with the poison plant while mowing the lawn. His arms and hands were wrapped in a boric acid solution.

It was too early to go for Eddie the morning two-year-old Steven woke me complaining about itching. He was covered in a rash, and John was away on TDY. Alarmed, I called a local doctor, dressed my child and self, and called the Foremans. "I must take Steven to the doctor. The other children are sleeping, but I will wake Johnny so he won't be frightened to find us gone. Will you keep an eye out?" Of course they would. I woke my six-year-old and explained.

"Steven's temporary rash will go away if you don't give him any more orange juice. He's allergic," the doctor said. In a matter of a few minutes, we were back home, but leaving sleeping children without attendance was a frightful feeling. I'm always reminded of this instance when a child is lost because it was left alone.

Life wasn't all about catastrophes. A joyous occasion was a visit by my brother, Frank, and his bride, Naomi. I worried about my culinary skills, because I had seen my new sister-in-law skillfully helping my mother in the kitchen.

It wasn't as though we never had guests. On one occasion, we invited a couple for dinner, and I served apple pie with a wedge of cheese. Apparently, the recipe didn't specify the thickness of a wedge. Cheese over-powered the dessert. It was dangerous to leave a cooking judgment to me, and, I thought, so much for trying to impress guests with magazine recipes.

But I gave myself credit for making tasty pies. Back then, even great crusts. Today, I still panic when someone is coming for dinner. I've learned to stick with ice cream toppings, use frozen piecrusts, and if the meal can't be made in an hour, forget it.

I don't recall how well I fed Frank and Naomi, but surprises always seemed a norm at our house. Consider the Halloween in DeRidder. I fashioned a cloth pumpkin on my sewing machine, stuffed Johnny into it and filled around him with tissue paper. Lindsey and Steven masqueraded in store-bought costumes. John took all three to "trick or treat" in the neighborhood.

While they rang doorbells, I wrapped the remainder of a lemon pie, left from dinner, and headed out to share it with the Kleuvers. Stepping from our patio into the night darkness beneath the pines, I crossed the Foremans' backyard when suddenly three figures loomed out of the ink-black right in front of me A blood-curdling scream escaped my lips. Pie soared into the air.

"Wow!" Holding his two little girls' hands, Jack Kleuver sounded unnerved. "I didn't mean to scare you. We were coming to trick or treat your house."

I calmed down, scooped up the pie plate and invited the girls for a treat.

Closing the door behind them, I started down the hall to check on David, the baby. Out of the corner of my eye, I caught sight of a small, rubber mouse lying against the baseboard. Had it been possible, I would have climbed the wall. Not since my teens had Halloween been so thrilling.

Entering David's room, I found him content as ever in his crib. A walk into this baby's presence always evoked a smile fit to melt any heart. On one occasion, however, his face puckered and nearly broke my heart. At six months of age, it was time to have his studio portrait taken. Eddie sat in the back seat, holding him as we rode into Leesville. Tired and sleepy by the time we arrived, the whole experience proved displeasing to him. He never reached the teary stage, but one picture shows his contorted face in a state of readiness. Soon the photographer was able to coax one big shy grin.

David was about seven months old when John was sent on an eight-week TDY at Fort Rucker, Alabama. He called. "I've rented three unfurnished rooms and a bath in the home of an elderly lady in the town of Ozark. I furnished them with rented beds, a dining table and chairs. You and the kids can come when you're ready."

It was early morning, and Gordon Foreman latched David's crib on the roof of our pink and white 1956 Rambler station wagon. We headed out around four o'clock. Traveling the gulf coastal route, I hoped to make the trip in a day, arriving in Ozark before nightfall. A friend warned me about women driving alone. "Wear a baseball cap with your hair pushed under it, and fall in behind an eighteen-wheeler." Other than the cap, I took her advice and followed along behind a truck until some place past Biloxi, Mississippi.

As Johnny and I talked about the beautiful scenery, Steven had a nature call. The same person who suggested the cap and eighteen-wheeler also suggested that I take an empty coffee can for just such an emergency. I offered the can to my small son.

"No! Not gonna use it. Cars see me." He glared at the cars stacked up behind us at a traffic light.

There wasn't a service station in sight, and I cajoled him. He had to make a decision or soil himself. Underway again, he used the can. Johnny rolled down the window and emptied it.

Imagine what plastered the back side of the car. What was I to do? David, lying in the front seat on a makeshift bed, began to whimper. He needed a diaper change. As soon as I could pull over and make him comfortable, I got out and cleaned the car. Had I known about the horrific rainstorm ahead of us, I would have let the downpour do the job.

Just before we reached Mobile, torrents came down in squalls. At the first available service station, I pulled beneath the canopy. An attendant emerged. "May I pull into one of your service bays until the rain's over? My baby's crib is getting wet." He agreed, and when the storm passed, I pulled out into a street that now resembled a canal. We followed behind other cars, through water up to the door line. It didn't occur to me that the engine might flood.

We arrived in Ozark around nine p.m. John had said he would wait for us at the home of Captain Dave Coors. I called from a public phone, and Dave's wife answered. "Dave and John have gone to a movie, but they should be home within minutes," she said.

Sitting in the car on the street in front of our rented space, the kids and I waited for John.

We settled into temporary living in Ozark. It turned out to be carefree. That may have been my first realization that the fewer possessions you have, the more free time you have. Housekeeping required dusting the few pieces of furniture, making the beds, sweeping out occasionally, and cooking. For the first time in years, I had time to read books. Our landlady left many classics in a large bookcase in the apartment.

Our children had scores of playmates in the neighborhood, all of whom found it hard to believe that we transplanted Arkansans had no taste for boiled peanuts. Are they eaten wet or dry?

Our landlady occupied the other side of the house, and one day she invited me to have tea with her and a visiting granddaughter. During the conversation, the dear old soul asked, "What do you think about Abraham Lincoln?"

"Along with President Roosevelt, I think he was among our greatest presidents."

The ninety-six-year-old went into spastic apoplexy. "Why that man destroyed the South! Worst thing that ever happened to this country. My daddy was a congressman. He took me to see him when I was four years old. That was an ugly man. Scary."

I don't recall being invited for tea again.

John's eight-week TDY duty ended, and we returned to DeRidder. But, we were not to be there long. My husband was ordered back to Fort Rucker for a two-year stint.

Knowing I would miss my faithful helper, I asked Eddie to move with us. "I surely would, Miz Foster, if I didn't have a husband."

We put our home in the hands of a realtor and headed back to Ozark in December 1956.

First Lieutenant John Foster, 1953, in Korea.

Lt. Colonel John Foster at Army Material Command, 1969,
Washington, D. C.

John Jr. (Johnny) Foster and Lindsey Ann Foster in a
Blue Bonnet patch, 1954, near Fort Hood, Texas.

Hurry, George (the time-set camera), Steve has a nature call.
Elizabeth, Lindsey, John, David, and Johnny dressed to
the nines for church, 1957, Dothan, Alabama.

The camel walla leads Elizabeth and Lindsey on a ride
along the Sandspit beach, near Karachi, 1959.

Johnny doesn't care much for the haircut ordeal even
if it is his regular barber, USA Charlie. Lindsey may be
sympathetic. In front of our villa, Karachi, Pakistan, 1960.

David, Steven, Lindsey, and Johnny dressed in
Sindhi wear in front of our villa in Karachi.

On the way to Agra, India, P. N. Singh (2nd from right) stopped
and asked the elephant owner to give Lindsey, Steven, Johnny, and
David a ride. The owner's wife and child stand behind Elizabeth.

A blurry image of John, Lindsey, Elizabeth, Johnny, Steven and David, taken by another visitor to the Taj Mahal, 1960. The reflecting pool is between our family and the monument in the background.

The faithful old 1955 Imperial and the new Nomad travel trailer, on the way to Edwards Air Force Base, California, 1963. Steven, David, Lindsey and Johnny stand beneath a Joshua Tree.

Our handsome dachshund, Skipper, born 1960 in Kharian,
Pakistan, died 1974 in Camp Springs, Maryland.

It's Sunday. Skipper, John, Steven, Johnny, David, Lindsey, and Elizabeth, Edwards Air Force Base California, 1965.

Oh, it's Sunday again! John, Steven, Elizabeth, David, Johnny, and Lindsey, 1970. Steven and David hold Skipper until George can snap the photo from the tripod.

"WE DON'T RENT TO PEOPLE WITH CHILDREN"

Another move just before Christmas was underway. Watching the van pull away from our Louisiana address, we loaded in the station wagon and started back to Alabama.

Settling into a rental apartment owned by the mayor of Ozark, we discovered the large complex housed many military families. Our stay was to be temporary while we searched for a house to rent.

We celebrated Lindsey's fifth birthday on December 23rd and went in search of a Christmas tree. The lots were almost empty, but with a small, lopsided fir, we returned to the apartment and tried to raise our spirits while decorating it with the kids' help. On Christmas Eve, Santa Claus arrived with fewer toys in his bag for the Foster children. Gift orders had gone out to Mrs. Claus before I packed travel bags for six people and waited for movers to invade our DeRidder home with boxes and crates.

Old Saint Nick felt safe, knowing our kids were too young to notice they had fewer gifts. And, they had no new friends with whom to compare.

After the holiday, we celebrated David's first birthday on December 28th. By then, I was more than ready to search for a permanent place to live. While the apartment was nice enough, it held one big surprise. Large numbers of people living in close proximity to each other gave rise to a culture of roaches. They traveled from one apartment to the next, looking for a crumb. Their numbers left me so paranoid I used a flyswatter on the pine knots in kitchen paneling. I could have sworn those knots moved.

We loaded up each day and went in search of a house. At each prospective place, we heard the same refrain. "We don't rent to people with children." Having exhausted the housing market in Ozark, we tried Dothan. Although the town was twenty miles from Fort Rucker, we met the same attitude.

This presented a case of having to purchase and make payments on two houses, or live with roaches. "We can't afford to buy another home and make two house payments," John said.

I was determined to have a home without roaches. "Yes we can. Even if it means eating bologna sandwiches every day until the DeRidder house sells."

Soon, we happened upon a newly constructed, three-bedroom house in Dothan. At this point, it didn't matter that the structure was totally devoid of any architectural character. Our new dwelling had beige asbestos siding with wrought iron trim around the covered front entrance, and an attached carport-utility room. Shelter without roaches meant happiness. What's more, we could handle the $10,000-quoted price. Its location, two blocks from an elementary school, was ideal because Johnny would start first grade in September.

It was the second home constructed in the development by Charlotte and Willard Farmer, the contractors. Upon completion of a unit, Willard's team of carpenters vacated, and Charlotte moved in to do all interior painting. She was a hard worker from McKeesport, Pennsylvania. Willard was a "good ole boy" from Alabama. They completed a house and lived in it while others were under construction.

We became good friends and played many games of Canasta with the Farmers.

Steven and David found a playmate in the little girl next door. She was the daughter of Willard's brother, Lawrence, and his wife, Martha. The Wilson children lived a block down Selma Street, and the Barber kids soon moved into a new house on a side street. We had a large backyard with a gym set and all these kids gathered there. Accidents were bound to happen with so many children about. More than one did. Lindsey and Steven gained permanent scars from being struck by moving swings.

John constructed a four-foot-high, cinder block fence down two sides of our back property. He capped the blocks with attractive, painted deck railing, and planted bamboo along the back yard to block unsightly scrub growth.

Johnny and Lindsey learned to ride their bikes on our neighborhood streets. John gave them starting pushes that often ended in skinned knees from contact with the pavement.

These activities allowed Saturdays to belong to me. If my husband was on TDY, I hired our regular grandmotherly babysitter to watch the children while I went to the hair salon and shopped for toys to bring home as rewards.

On one of my Saturday shopping excursions, I walked along a department store counter, intent on making selections when I looked up to see a face not two feet away, staring back at me. "Oh, please excuse me," I said. Then, I realized it was my own reflection in a mirror, and I had begged excuse of myself. Embarrassed, I glanced around. Had anyone witnessed the scene?

More often than not I came home disappointed after shopping for children's books. I had experienced the scarcity of such books in other places, and was convinced that 1950s' publishers didn't consider children's exposure to reading.

September approached. Johnny missed most of the kindergarten year. He had attended three months in DeRidder, but classes were filled by the time we moved to Dothan. School opened, and he trudged down the block with the older Barber kids to his second day of first grade. He kept glancing back and waving. I wanted to cry.

Not long into the school term, his first grade teacher called me for a conference. "He's daydreaming," she said. "Looking out the window all the time instead of doing his work."

I knew our kid was smart enough. "He does his homework. Maybe he's bored."

She disallowed this in no uncertain terms, but I shall always believe that young woman, in her first year of teaching, made school an unpleasant experience for our child. Nevertheless, he made average grades throughout his educational years despite numerous moves to many places in the middle of school terms.

I don't remember the process by which Lindsey was selected for Romper Room, but I took her to the television studio in Dothan each day. She loved being on the stage, and I enjoyed watching her participate on our TV set.

All too soon, our children anticipated another Santa visit. When holiday shopping was completed and toys hidden away, John and I took them downtown to see jolly old Saint Nick. We visited several stores, each of which had their own uniformed fellow. Afterwards, we walked down the sidewalk to the car when Johnny looked up at me. "None of them was Santa Claus."

"What makes you think that?"

"'Cause they aren't the same. Besides, their beards weren't real."

What do you do when you have a doubter and three little believers? Back home and alone with him, I explained, "Santa Claus is the spirit of Christmas, and spirits are never seen. They're like angels. That's why he has helpers, like those men in Santa suits." I asked him to not tell his siblings or any other child there wasn't a Santa. If he did I never knew, but to this day, Johnny doesn't appreciate the "lie" surrounding Santa Claus.

Our son was astute for his young years. On leaving the movie theater one evening, we walked past the police station. Stopping, I pointed out the men who would help anyone in need.

Little did I know that on a Saturday afternoon he would have a need. Mrs. Barber invited him to go to the matinee with her boys. Her older children were to look after my seven-year-old.

An hour or so later, we answered the doorbell. A policeman stood on our porch. "Are you Mrs. Foster? Do you have a son named Johnny?"

Hearing positive responses, the lawman pointed to his vehicle. "Johnny's in my patrol car."

The Barber kids left him alone in the theater to go to the lobby for popcorn. Our son must have panicked, but at least he had the good sense to go to the police station. He said he was lost and gave his name and address.

Clearly, our children were the center of my life. There were times when I wondered if ever again I would be able to conduct an adult conversation.

Our second Easter in Dothan arrived. We always decked out for church on this holy day. John and the boys in suits, Lindsey and me in hats, which she refused to keep on her head. The notation on the back of one photo reads: "Easter, 1958, Dothan, Alabama. All are cute as bugs' ears." Johnny wore a pink jacket over long pants. Pink for males was big that year. Lindsey had on a frilly dress and headwear. Steven and David were in striped seersucker suits with short pants, hand-me-downs from Johnny.

One Sunday, Charlotte invited us for ice cream made in a hand-turned freezer. We sat in the Farmers' back yard as she warned about a beehive in a large oak tree. Suddenly, the pests swarmed down on Johnny. He endured numerous stings that sent us running for ice. Soon, his unpleasant pain was lost to the soothing taste of delicious homemade ice cream.

It was our fate that good times ended all too soon. Johnny began second grade and at September's end, his dad had orders to Pakistan.

"Where in the world is Pakistan?" I asked. John and I were too involved in the dating game to notice the Muslim and Hindu uprisings and the British partition of Pakistan from India in the late Forties. We took down the atlas and scanned information about the country in the encyclopedia recently purchased from a door-to-door salesman.

Soon, a letter came from our sponsoring family in Karachi, telling us what to expect and which necessities to ship to that faraway land.

The kids and I began weekly trips to the Fort Rucker hospital for all the many shots necessary to reside in a third-world nation. We went early in the morning so I could return Johnny to his classes. One morning after our trip to the base, I put the Rambler in PARK and warned Lindsey to not allow two-year-old David behind the wheel. He liked to play with the gearshift.

Johnny and I walked up the sidewalk and into the principal's office where an aide spoke on the phone. We stood waiting for someone's attention when I heard a scream. Leaving Johnny, I tore out of the building, only to be passed by the school janitor. He ran after the car as it headed for an intersection about a block away. Lindsey ran alongside the open front door, trying to hold David inside the car.

When the car was stopped, Steven was nowhere to be seen. Looking up the street where the car had been parked, I spotted him walking toward us. He had bailed out the back window of the station wagon. My heart still races when I think of that potential disaster.

Finally, all the required inoculations were finished, our passport pictures were made, and John arranged for a month's leave. While the house in DeRidder had sold about a year after we moved, here we were again, leaving the Dothan house without a buyer. The Farmers offered to handle it as a rental, and to sell it if a buyer came along.

Thoroughly seasoned by now, I had come to realize that contentment with where you were didn't count for much when you lived a military life. In late November 1958, we bid Fort Rucker and Dothan friends goodbye, and left our happy little Alabama home. Most of our household items went into storage. The rest was crated and bound for shipment to Karachi, Pakistan.

We traveled to Arkansas to have Christmas with our families, whom we would not see for another two years. In Lewisville, Johnny visited a second grade class to keep him current in school. During that time, playing his first acting role as a tin soldier in a school performance gave him a thrill.

John's leave ended, and sometime before New Year's Day, 1959, we departed our hometown en route for Fort Hamilton, New York.

TRAVEL TO A FARAWAY COUNTRY

On the trip to Fort Hamilton, New York, we came upon snow-cover in Tennessee, and dealt with it all the way to Coraopolis, a suburb of Pittsburgh, Pennsylvania. We stopped there for a brief visit with my aunt's family. The rest of the journey was just as arduous, for the northeastern seaboard was snowed-over.

Arriving at Fort Hamilton, we checked into one room of a barracks shared with dozens of other families awaiting flights to overseas assignments. While I attempted to keep four snowbound youngsters corralled within our small confines, John arranged to ship our car and attend to other pressing matters.

It was maddening, and I no longer tried to anticipate what might lie ahead. I was more than ready to start the new adventure when the airport runways finally cleared. On a dark rainy evening, we loaded onto a military bus. It took us to La Guardia International Airport. Soaring away into the night on a Pan Am flight, I woke sometime later in Newfoundland, where the plane sat down to refuel. The next day, we landed at Rhein Mein Air Force Base, Germany, and bussed over snow-covered streets to a hotel on the base.

Again, weather held up our departure for Pakistan. The hotel, a modern high-rise, served as the guesthouse for families with overseas assignments, as well as other guests. Lindsey was afraid of the elevator and had to be coaxed to enter, but Johnny rode it up and down. He had been penned in for many days, and I couldn't be too concerned for waiting users stranded on their floors.

Departing snowy Germany in early January, we flew out on another Pan Am plane. During the long flight, our young children—Johnny approached nine, Lindsey was six, Steven four, David three—were content to use coloring books, read, and sleep or peer out the plane's windows. David's furry monkey, Zippy, kept him company.

After many hours on the plane, disembarking at the Beirut, Lebanon, airport in the middle of the night turned into an unnerving experience. Apparently, the recent 1957 Israeli-Arab War was still fresh in Arab minds. Herded from the plane into a roomful of armed guards with rifles held at the ready, we guarded our four children against any quick movements. Under those conditions, airport hospitality refreshed us with complimentary glasses of orange juice.

Back on the plane my edginess eroded, and I slept through the rest of the night. Awaking in the morning, I looked through the porthole as air mile after air mile, wave after wave of nothing but sand passed far below us. We made our way over the Iranian desert, and as midday approached, we neared Pakistan.

FLIGHT FROM POLAR WEATHER TO HADES-LIKE HEAT

Around noon, the plane let down at Karachi International Airport. Other passengers seemed as antsy as we were to dismount. Coming to a standstill on the tarmac, the stewardess announced, "Keep your seats. People are coming aboard to spray the cabin against any germs you might have brought into the country. It will be thirty minutes before you can debark."

Some returning passengers turned to laugh at our puzzled faces. We had read information that led us to think we should be the ones to worry about germs.

Once detoxification had supposedly killed our microorganisms, our kids and belongings were gathered up, and we entered the line moving toward the exit. On the ramp, a sudden blast of hot air and dust seared our faces. Off in the distance, white-clad sweepers were in a seemingly fruitless pursuit of swirling sand on the runway.

Dust took our breaths, and the hellish heat of the Karachi day penetrated our clothing. John wore a winter uniform. I was in a woolen suit, and the kids had on winter jackets. It was as though in a night and day we had flown from the North Pole into Hades.

Captain Bill Scott, our military sponsor, led us through customs. Then, we loaded into Mr. Deigner's carryall. The civilian head of the motor pool for Trans-East District Corps of Engineers (T-EDCE) drove us to the Scotts' house.

A hoard of people had gathered there to greet us. All belonged, in one way or another, to T-EDCE, of which John was now a part.

We sat in the Scotts' living room with an enthusiastic group. Truth be known, they came to welcome John, the soon-to-be pilot of a twin-engine Beechcraft assigned to T-EDCE.

The plane, flown by other Army pilots, was on the way to Karachi. My husband's assignment was to provide an improved means of transportation back and forth from south to north Pakistan for civil engineers and military officers. Those wayfarers had their fill of riding rail cars eight hundred miles one-way with Pakistanis crowding or clinging to the sides or sitting on top of slow-moving trains while clutching all varieties of animals and fowl. The plane would take T-EDCE men on frequent flights to Multan, the Punjab, Quetta, Rawalpindi, Peshawar, Lahore, all northern destinations in about two to four hours or less.

Now, after twenty-four hours on a fast-moving plane, there I sat in the Scotts' home, struggling with jet lag while trying to be attentive to a roomful of kind people. All I could think about was a hot shower and two or three days in bed. Nodding to their words, I propped my head on my hand, and strained to keep my eyes open and appear as if every utterance was interesting.

As always our children joined other kids, including the Scotts' three and the Benson and DuPlantis' five youngsters, as if they had always known them. All fit into the same age range.

At last, people began to drift away, and a glimpse of my hands revealed a missing wedding band. I recalled washing in the plane's lavatory and removing my ring to apply lotion.

Mr. Deigner went into action. "I'll call the airport and have them check out the plane." That done, he had us load back into the carryall to be driven to our new residence. It was then we discovered David's Zippy had been left on the plane, too. Mr. Deigner said not to worry. He would ask about the toy monkey when the airport contacted him about the ring.

He fell in behind Bill and Irene Scott's station wagon and headed for our compound.

A STEP BACK IN TIME

Our upper-class villa rested on a slight rise inside a compound wall on Karachi's northwestern side, known as the PECHS ("peaches") District.

In 1959, Karachi, then the capital of Pakistan, was home to nearly a million people. The British partitioned the Muslim nation consisting of two states, West Pakistan and East Pakistan (now Bangladesh), from India in 1947. The settlement of a religious problem left India largely a Hindu country. The Thar Dessert, home of the Sindhi tribe, stretched from Karachi over a large distance between the city and the town of Multan to the northeast. The Arabian Sea bordered Pakistan on the south, Iran west, Afghanistan northwest, China northeast, and India on the east.

Dreigh Road, one of the main arteries into downtown Karachi, ran two blocks below our sand-colored stucco villa. Houses lay in place with no rhythm or reason. The Scotts said a former Pakistani president owned the compound next door to us. True or not, we never knew.

They toured us around our sprawling, new home and introduced two of our eight servants —cook-bearer, hamal, ayah, indoor sweeper, outdoor sweeper, mali, chowidar, and the dhobi.

Khan, the cook-bearer, supervised all of them, and in the beginning, he slept in the servant quarters connected to the back of the house. Tush (Tosh) the chowidar (chog-i-dar), guarded us by securing the gate and walking inside the compound wall at night. Our mali (molly/ gardener) watered and tended plants during the day and slept in the servant quarters at night.

We spent our first night sleeping on Corps of Engineer-issued charpai (charpoys), cots with rope supports for a thin mattress.

Waking next morning, we found Khan and other servants going about their duties.

Diliwar (Del-i-war), the hamal (ha-mal), assisted Khan in food preparations and serving our meals in the dining room. He cleared the table and washed dishes beneath the spigot rising up from the concrete kitchen floor. Between those chores, he made beds, dusted and polished.

Diliwar's wife, Violet, was our ayah or nursemaid. She kept up with our four young kids.

Twice a day, morning and afternoon, the indoor sweeper, Bashira (Ba-shir-ra), came to treat the terrazzo floors. He did this on hands and knees with a kerosene rag mop. The floors shone like newly minted coins. He also cleaned the two bathrooms. In the caste system, he was known as an "untouchable."

The outdoor sweeper came twice a day to clean the compound grounds with a short-handled straw broom.

The dhobi (dough-be) came once a week to stomp the laundry in the bathtub with his bare feet. It dried on outdoor lines, then he ironed each piece. We purchased a wringer washing machine, but it was many weeks before it arrived in our household crates. The car would be weeks arriving from the States, too.

That first morning in Karachi, Irene Scott came early to check that all the house servants had shown up for duty, and to take me to the Empress Market. I still suffered from jet lag, and her planned market adventure proved unwise.

Empress Market covered several acres in downtown Karachi. Fish lay open on counters. Nude chickens, geese and ducks dangled from strings, and live ones squabbled in coops. Halves of whole beef, lamb, and pork hung from wires and small meat portions were openly displayed on counters. All attracted zillions of flies.

Luscious fruits and vegetables of all varieties tempted one to buy. Sweet smelling mangos, papaya, apricots, and sugar cane cut like celery sticks, filled bins. There were other exotic fruits as well as the kinds commonly sold in the States.

Flies feasting on unattractive meat, the mingling fish, fowl, and fruit odors overwhelmed me. Apparently, Irene's constitution was stronger than mine. She found my predicament funny. Later, when I had time to acclimate to our new way of life, I occasionally went to Empress Market.

Eating raw vegetables proved dangerous for Americans. Khan was responsible for making them edible when cooked, and the water potable for us. He rode his bicycle some distance to the market to buy our produce. Then, beneath the kitchen spigot, he washed vegetables and fruits in Tide detergent. After thoroughly cleansing, he soaked them in iodine-infused water before cooking. We couldn't risk eating lettuce, celery or raw carrots even after a detergent-iodine treatment. Consuming uncooked vegetables and drinking unboiled water resulted in the "Karachi trots," or "GI Karachi," as some referred to the dysentery. Khan cooked all of our food with the exception of fruits. They had to be soaked and peeled.

Karachi's leaky water and sewer pipes ran parallel, allowing water and sewage to meet and mix. Every other day, Khan boiled and stored water for drinking. Some went into a Scotch bottle in the bathroom for brushing our teeth. Several days a week, he kneaded bread dough on a small kitchen table and baked it in the kerosene range's oven.

The mali (molly) created a pretty garden array through which to welcome our guests. The climate was temperate-mild, so flowering plants grew in colorful profusion. Bougainvillea climbed most compound walls.

Sometimes Tush, the chowidar, kept us awake at night when reading aloud in Urdu from his Bible. All of our servants were of the Christian faith.

We paid one hundred rupees per month for the services of all eight servants, and bought the men's western-style uniforms—long cotton white pants and short sleeve shirts. One rupee amounted to twenty-five cents in American currency in 1959. Those Pakistanis wealthy enough to hire servants weren't happy with Americans' over-indulging payment system.

We entered Johnny in the last half of the second grade and Lindsey in kindergarten.

In the beginning, I had two overriding concerns, servants and distance. As any ordinary American housewife might have been, at first I was overwhelmed by eight servants, but soon found Khan quite capable of keeping our household running smoothly. And, our villa, surrounded by Pakistanis, was some distance from any of the other four thousand Americans (according to the U. S. Embassy) residing in Karachi at the time. Although we had no contact with our Pakistani neighbors, they presented no problems.

The Corps of Engineers issued furniture for our house: charpoys, bureaus and chairs for bedrooms, seating and tables for the living room, and table, chairs, and dish cabinet for the dining room. We expected our Rambler station wagon, bedding, Amana freezer, linens, kitchenware, and the children's toys and gym set to arrive from the States.

Military and civilian Corps personnel had "carryall" vehicles and drivers assigned to them. Our first morning in Karachi, John's driver, Madar (Ma-dar), arrived to take him to Quamar House, the engineer district headquarters. The Beechcraft's home, when it arrived, would be Dreigh Road Airport. Madar would take John to the airport on days he had to fly.

Our car arrived in March. Every day until then, Irene or one of the few other seasoned Corps wives, brave enough to drive in Karachi, came to take me out. Bent on introducing me to Pakistani culture, we went to the downtown bazaars, to coffee klatsches, or to the commissary.

Fortunately, a stateside-like commissary provided food for the "American community." Frozen meats and fowl came from Denmark, canned goods and other staples from the States. All essentials, with the exception of eggs, bread and pasturized milk. We used powdered milk, and Khan stood in line for hours at Empress Market to get four to six eggs.

One day at the commissary, I witnessed an "ugly American" scene. A woman from the States "mouthed off" to a Pakistani bag person as he loaded groceries into her car. She may have had reason to complain, but to make a commotion with someone who could not speak English was uncalled for. He didn't need to understand what she said to know she scorned him.

We had been in Karachi a few days when Lieutenant Werner Weiss, the other engineer district pilot, arrived in Pakistan. My husband received word that the Beechcraft plane had been flown as far as Pisa, Italy. He and Lieutenant Weiss would have to go to Pisa and fly it to Karachi. At the end of our first week in the country, they left for Italy.

During John's weeklong absence, the children and I were alone in a strange country with an unknown man, Khan, in the servants' quarters, and another patrolling our grounds. I moved the kids' charpoys into my bedroom and tried to sleep beneath the smelly camel hair blanket.

A kerosene space heater, required against January's night chill, emitted its own noxious odor.

And if that wasn't enough to keep sleep away, there were the night sounds drifting from Dreigh Road up the hill to our villa. Donkeys trotted on belled legs, jingling like Santa's reindeer. Camels, water buffaloes and elephants plodded along, making cowbell clangs. All were on their way with produce and wares for the morning opening of Empress Market. Each animal made its own distinct sound in the otherwise silent, sleepless night. Lying awake, smelling the odors, and listening to the noises, I repeated, "There goes a donkey, an elephant. That's a camel." The sounds soon became familiar and no longer interfered with sleep.

On the Beechcraft's return flight, Lieutenant Weiss, an American with a Jewish sounding name, had reason to be uneasy when he and John landed at Arab airports, such as Beirut, Lebanon, to refuel the plane.

The weeklong trip ended, and John began making flights to the Corps of Engineer sights situated at various Pakistani locations. Many times he was away for two or more days. On trips to Peshawar, he picked up a case of twelve dozen beautiful eggs to distribute. Soon, he became known as the "egg man."

We settled comfortably into our new home and even accepted the harmless lizards that climbed our indoor walls. To the Corps-issued furniture, we added cane-woven seating for the screened porches and had cushion covers made with "Foster" batik-printed in Urdu (Ur-du), the Pakistani language. Bright blue drapery was fashioned to dress our windows, and we went to the city jail to purchase beautiful cotton rugs, hand-woven by the prisoners.

Directly behind our compound wall, a great open space spread out in a desert floor of sand dotted with scrub bushes. A well-worn, well-traveled, pedestrian path crossed it to Dreigh Road.

Soon we came to accept the trail scene of Pakistani men dressed in white sharliwars (sharl-i-wars, pajama-like wear) and squatting to heed a call of nature. Resembling great white birds, they didn't bother to get behind a bush.

Like many cultures, Pakistanis were of many creeds and colors. Lower caste men wore the sharliwars, a white cotton tunic over white, full-gathered bottoms held at the waist by drawstrings and banded snugly at the ankle. Their women covered with solid dyed or print tunics over gathered pajama pants and sometimes a head cover.

Some husbands required wives to wear black or blue burkas—a one piece head cover and robe with open slits for their eyes. Only hands and sandaled feet were exposed. A dark burka robe might be worn with a loose scarf for head cover and to pull across the face below the eyes.

Upper-class men dressed in western-style suits and shoes or western casual. Some wore lamb's wool Jinnah caps as seen on Afghanistan's President Karsai. Their wives and daughters wore short-sleeved mid-drift tops over the upper torso, then wrapped in a colorful sari. The sari, a long piece of silk or sheer fabric wide enough to reach from waist to ankle, circled tight enough around waists to hold in place the folded pleats or gathers tucked in front. It formed a full-length skirt with enough end left to cross the chest and throw over one shoulder. The mid-drift top allowed a small area of the back waist to show the light skin tone of the higher caste. Graceful Pakistani women appeared to float when walking. Sandals were primary footwear for everyone.

Because of our revealing dress, American women were warned, "Don't go alone into downtown Karachi. Men may pinch you." Was that wishful thinking on someone's part? Sometimes idle men commented and laughed as we passed by them in our dresses, but there was never a pinch. Overall, Americans and Pakistanis dealt with each other in a congenial and friendly manner.

The kids soon discovered playmates across the street. Zeekie and his younger sister were children of a Pakistani father, who had rescued their Polish mother from a German concentration camp at the end of World War II.

Monkey wallas (venders) showed up at the villa within a week or so of our arrival. While they cranked organs, their primates performed for the kids. Snake wallas charmed cobras with flutes, and mongooses kept the vipers in their basket. Horse and camel wallas offered rides. After our children enjoyed a show, the walla asked for a "buckshee" (a rupee).

One morning Mrs. Clark dropped me at home after we had been to a coffee. I leaned on the car door, talking with her. When I turned to enter our gate, a young walla had a charmed cobra no more than two feet behind me. Screaming, I jumped back into the car. "No, no. We don't want a performance." It took at least ten minutes to convince him.

In a short time, we became acquainted with all our fellow Corps and military families. There were frequent parties, and we became a close-knit family of Patersons, DiGiacomos, Bectells, DuPlantises, Richards, Ghormleys, Bensons, Haags, Scotts, and others.

In Karachi, we had to create our own entertainment. Told to bring cocktail dresses, I purchased a new one before leaving the States. The style was satin overlaid with net and under layers of crinoline. It was bright red, not my favorite color. At the first party we attended, one of the guys stumbled and fell into my arms, spilling his drink all over the dress. I wasn't fond of the dress anyway, and never wore it again.

The first six months we were in Karachi, Colonel Frederick Clark commanded the engineering district. He and Mrs. Clark had a daughter our Johnny's age. After they returned to the States, he became a three-star general and engineer commissioner of the District of Columbia. Years later, John and I met him at the Pentagon. Colonel and Mrs. Northington replaced Colonel Clark's family.

Sergeant Lloyd Haag, his wife, Joyce, daughter Judy, and son Paul arrived a few weeks behind us. Lloyd, the Beechcraft mechanic, kept the plane in the air. He also managed Salateen, the clubhouse, and procured movies we enjoyed on Salateen's rooftop. Not long after the Haags landed in Pakistan, Joyce learned she was pregnant. Both she and Irene Scott gave birth to babies in a Karachi hospital.

Shortly after our arrival, the embassy ushered Colonel and Mrs. Dryer out of the country for their protection. Mrs. Dryer ran over and killed a Pakistani youth on a bicycle. Under the Muslim belief in an "eye for an eye," Mrs. Dryer was in eminent danger.

Such an accident was bound to occur in a city of close to a million people and only one traffic light. Two months after we arrived, twelve more lights were installed and traffic deaths decreased, according to a city newspaper article I sent in a letter. Karachi streets presented all sorts of moving hazards for drivers and the downtown police who directed traffic. Driving on the left side of the street, a leftover British influence, was another experience for Americans.

Few Corps wives drove in Karachi. John rarely took the wheel, sometimes to our beach house or to parties, so it fell to me to do most of our family transporting. It took confidence and courage to dodge cattle, goat and sheep herds marked with identifying paint spots, and belled and floral-decorated camels, donkeys and elephants pulling carts. There were water buffalo, rickshaws, scooters, motorcycles and bicycles, automobiles, and a horde of people on foot. All distractions.

I had plenty of time to drive places. With servants to fill every need, there was little left to do. I took the kids to play times and spent hours with friends, shopping the commissary and brass and copper bazaars, and sending photos and descriptive letters back to Arkansas.

With our lack of physical activity, five Corps wives took up twice-weekly lessons in classical Indian dance. Rafi Anwar instructed us at the American Embassy. Four of the ladies lasted only a few months, but I persevered.

The dhersi (der-si/tailor) made my costume from a white silk sari embroidered throughout and bordered in gold and red threads. The mid-drift top had three-quarter sleeves, jewel neckline and snaps fastened the front. Ballooned pants snugged around the ankles, similar to the Sharliwar. Dancers wore head beads, bracelets, and ankle bells.

In 1960, a month or so before we left Pakistan to return to the States, Rafi brought his musical combo players with tabla drums, sitar and one other string instrument to the house to make a recording, so that I could keep up the dance. Needless to say, I didn't. However, I did perform for the last party at our house before leaving the country.

When we arrived back in Arkansas, I demonstrated some of the moves for my parents and modeled the bare mid-drift costume.

"You mean you belly danced?" Dad was aghast.

I explained the dance was performed on bare feet and the moves were nothing like a belly dance. "It's more like a mix of graceful, upper body hula shifts and Cossack squats."

Corps wives also performed service projects. The embassy furnished reconstituted powdered milk for Pakistani students. I held an office in our wives' club that took turns with other organized American groups in making milk deliveries to the schools. We found students seated on row after row of long benches with no back rests, chanting their lessons, learning by rote, much like the Iraqi Madrasahs (Ma-drasas) seen today on television.

For most Pakistanis, life posed hardships. Some photos we mailed home depicted Pakistani women seated on the ground at construction sites, beating large rocks into small ones. Others showed men mixing cement to be sent hand-over-hand by the pan-full along a line of women until it reached a ladder. At the ladder, women passed the pan to the top of the building to form flat roofs. Menial labor gained the workers a rupee per day.

Many such sights left us astounded. The working class had stamina and endurance. On the other hand, there were those who were totally reliant on others. Such as the holy man who lived on the bridge spanning the harbor to the port side of town. One day on the way to the commissary, the kids noticed him. One yelled, "Mom, that man's naked!" He walked up and down the bridge, or sat or slept on a dirty cloth. Wrapping himself in the dingy cloth on cooler days, the filthy, straggly-haired man was a guru to those who brought him food.

One of the most intriguing religious entities in Karachi was the Parsi community, a Zoroastrian sect. Parsees descended from Persian refugees who fled Moslem persecutions in the seventh and eighth centuries. Their principle belief system, contained in the Zend-Avesta, included an afterlife and a continuous struggle between the universal spirit of good (Or-mazd) and the spirit of evil (Ahriman), with good ultimately prevailing.

A lighted torch in the Parsi temple was never extinguished, and most peculiar was their method of disposing of the dead. Corpses were placed on open platforms to be picked clean of flesh by vultures. After which, the bones were collected and taken to the ocean. Our villa was some distance away, but on some days we could see vultures soaring above the platforms.

We had been in Karachi about two months, long enough to observe many of the customs, when Captain Boyce Buckner, Bonnie, and their two sons, Gary and Kevin, arrived. Boyce, also an Army pilot, was sent north to the Kharian Army Cantonment to be an assistant to Colonel Lewis, the project engineer.

Kharian was one of T-EDCE's military assistance and advisory (MAAG) projects. The cantonment was under construction and modeled after Fort Hood's barracks, water wells, parade grounds, motor parks, and officers' quarters. Large refrigerated storage rooms were added. Why refrigerated rooms? They weren't necessary, unless our government thought Pakistanis were going to change their custom of killing animals and consuming the meat the same day. Like at the Empress Market, meat wasn't refrigerated. Pakistanis at Kharian used the cooled rooms to store water.

Another mistake at the Kharian base centered around the positioning of cantonment toilets. Commodes were placed so that users faced Mecca, a no-no in Muslim religious tradition.

We sponsored the Buckners, and before they flew off to Kharian, we had them to dinner. Khan brought a turkey to the table to carve. I gasped when he cut into the cooked bird and pulled the bag of giblets from the cavity. Then, Diliwar came bearing a bowl of grass green, mashed potatoes garnished at the peak with a pimento-stuffed olive on a toothpick.

We said nothing, for Khan took pride in his creations.

Dinner ended with Boyce spraying an aerosol can of dessert topping across the table. Who wouldn't become lifelong friends after sharing such laughs?

Shortly after John flew the Buckners to Kharian, we experienced our first monsoon. Once or twice a year, rains came to Karachi. In April, the deluge sent water gushing from our flat roof, down the wide stairway separating the living room on the left and a bedroom on the right. It flooded the long screened porch and ran into two more bedrooms. That storm washed away the back compound wall and knocked out power to our large Amana freezer. I saved frozen food through friends' generosity in sharing their freezer space.

Monsoons could last a couple of days or up to a week. That one caught John on a flight homeward. It was unusual for him to fly in after dark, but on that night the hour was late, rain was heavy and the lightening fierce. In a worried state, I waited up. Finally, a plane was heard to buzz low overhead around nine p.m. It sounded like the Beechcraft, but I couldn't be sure. It was two a.m. when Madar brought him from the airport. "The carryall flooded on the way home, and we sat on the side of the road, waiting until Madar could start it again," John explained.

Many Pakistanis died in that monsoon. Thousands, who lived on mud flats in structures thrown together out of scrap lumber, metal or even cardboard, once again found themselves homeless. A resilient people, they went about rebuilding their hottels (hote-uls).

We, too, needed to be resilient. Accidents always seemed to occur on a weekend, and so it was on a Sunday that Johnny and Lindsey climbed upon the pump shed roof.

A tanker truck of water arrived weekly at our villa from what source, only-God-knew. The water went into an underground holding vat beneath the pump shed situated on a concrete slab outside the kitchen door. Then it was pumped from the vat into a metal tank above the pump house and gravity fed it into the house.

Our adaptability in a foreign country was tested that Sunday when Lindsey peered over the edge of the pump shed and fell onto the concrete below. Johnny screamed for us.

When we reached her, one side of her face was already black. She wasn't unconscious, but kept falling asleep. I ran across the street to our Pakistani neighbor's and phoned one of several doctors assigned to the embassy clinic. "Doctor Winters, our daughter fell eight feet onto concrete. Can you come?"

He called the Seventh Day Adventist Hospital, and John drove us there. X-rays showed no concussion, but she was hospitalized overnight for observation. I stayed with her, and next day Lindsey was released with a dark green bruise.

Another unpleasant incident occurred one afternoon when the kids and I returned from a playtime visit. Full of excitement, Khan met us at the front door. "Memsahib, this man came in the house to take things." He babbled on about the man who wakened him from his nap, and whom he had tied up and stood guard over.

"Since the man didn't steal anything, Khan, we should let him go." I had heard tales about the treatment of prisoners in Karachi jails.

"No, Memsahib, he is a no-good man. He will break-in again."

Telephone service was so poor that Americans didn't bother with phones. Again, I ran to our Pakistani neighbor and asked to ring John at Quamar House. He reported the incident to Captain Bennie Benson, a criminal investigator in the Provost Marshal's Office.

As John and Bennie drove from Quamar House to our place, Khan stood guard. The poor fellow pled to be released as he was loaded into the vehicle to be hauled away. It was more than likely he had a hungry family. I never learned his fate, nor did I wish to know.

Added to the criminal element were the beggars. Common to downtown Karachi streets, they sometimes came to our compound gate. A few were unable to speak because their tongues were cut out during the Hindu-Muslim uprisings in the '40s.

Some parents blinded or maimed their infants and carried or led them about begging in bazaar areas. Others maimed themselves. One day, a man on the street approached John and me. Holding out his forearm, he gestured at a deep self-inflicted wound. He had gouged out the flesh to the bone. "Please, Sahib, Memsahib, buckshees." His impassioned plea prompted my husband to lead me away.

" If you give to one, soon many surrounded you." However pitiful, we had been warned not to give money to any of them.

Many sights evoked pity, such as nude babies, sometimes with only short pullover tops above bare bottoms, crawling about on dirt floors of hottels. Flies sipped moisture from their eyes, noses and mouths. The poorest of families washed their clothing and bathed in mud holes where water buffalo and other animals drank and rolled about. Water was a precious commodity.

Most days, we contended with a desert sun. American mothers kept their children indoors in the afternoon. Because of a limited power system, we had restricted use of the air conditioner, only between the hours of ten a.m. to ten p.m. A sea breeze usually cooled the nights.

School operated half-days due to the heat. The regular term ended in May, and Johnny was promoted to the third grade. It was hot as Hades, and we joined a pool of four other families in renting a beach house. At times, ten to fifteen children built sand castles, combed the Sandspit beach for shells, played with beach balls or enjoyed the warm water. Under the Pakistani sun, Lindsey and I tanned a deep shade of brown, leaving us to resemble the natives.

Once a year after nightfall, giant female sea turtles clambered some twenty yards upon the beach to lay and cover their eggs with sand. Crowds showed up for the annual event. After they propagated their species, children rode the reptilians back into the water's edge. Baby turtles hatched and made their own way down to the sea.

Blue bottles (jelly fish) populated the water, and Johnny burned like fire from a sting. We had only a raw onion at the beach house to rub on him until we could get home.

Getting to the beach house meant enduring unpleasant odors. "Hold your noses. 'Stinky corner' is just ahead." Our kids chimed in anticipation of reaching the sharp curve where raw sewage ran in a stream on its way to the ocean. In the area of stinky corner, women and children kept bony cattle herds and picked up cow manure to make patties for fuel. They cooked chapatis (cha-patis, flat bread) on a rock heated with cow patties. If we took photos of the women, it had to be from a distance, for photographing Muslim women was frowned upon.

Boyce Buckner often flew from Kharian with John to Karachi and stayed with us. A camel hayride party had been fun, but I had never ridden the smelly animal. On one of Boyce's visits we took him to the beach house. A walla with three camels found us on the beach and offered rides. All of us got aboard, a feat in itself. The dromedary knelt on front legs and the walla helped Lindsey board. With a great deal of assistance, I positioned myself to swing a leg over our camel's saddle behind her.

The critter raised up, heaving us upward and forward. The ride was like sitting atop an undulating wave.

Despite the hazards of stingers, tanning sun, and stinky corner's awful odor, beach activities provided many pleasurable hours.

Pakistan's climate required light clothing. If the boys needed new outfits, I pulled out the Sears-Roebuck Catalog and sent off an order. Sometimes I ordered fabric for Lindsey and me, as well, or purchased it from a bazaar. Then I searched the pages for dress styles. Pakistani preference for bright colors and unusual mixing of shades demanded a leap in taste.

When fabric came in the mail, I sent word to the dhersi (der-si). He came to the house with the sewing machine head and a white cloth in his hand. Spreading the cloth on the floor, he sat and studied the catalog styles I had chosen. Without taking a measurement or drawing a pattern, he cut the material. Then, cross-legged on the spread cloth before his treadle-less machine, he fashioned new dresses by spinning the wheel.

Our first summer in Karachi ended, and the regular school term was to open in late August, but it was delayed by an outbreak of polio among Americans. I shuttled our servants back and forth to the Embassy clinic for the needed vaccine.

School opened in September, and Johnny began the third grade. I wrote to his grandparents that he thought of a thousand things he'd rather be doing than going to school. Most of the teachers were housewives without qualifications to teach. Johnny didn't care for his third grade teacher, and often complained about her.

Lindsey left the much-lauded English kindergarten and entered first grade. She liked school and came home full of excitement. Steven entered kindergarten, and I tried to send David, but he would have none of it. Word came that he cried. When I retrieved him at the end of the week, he whimpered, "I just want to be home with you." He wasn't ready for school.

Parents took turns riding the bus that delivered children to their schools. If it broke down, the driver got out and cranked until it started again. Steven laughed at the cranking and imitated it. They were fond of the little green bus.

The school term moved into the fall of 1959, and a heated October presented a sandstorm to remember. Somehow the fine dust sifted through windows and doors into our houses, discoloring everything orange. We learned this was normal for the hottest month of the year, and wondered what the spring monsoon season would bring.

Like the weather and some people of any nationality, Pakistanis could be seen committing cruel acts. Khan wasn't a cruel person, but he sparred with the brown, thick-furred mutt we acquired. We named our small puppy Pices (Pi-cees) for the Pakistani coin of least value. Khan's rough playfulness caused the dog to develop meanness and to bite. We asked him to take it to his hottel, or give it to someone.

One day on a trip to town, I saw a cart tipped backwards and the little donkey left to dangle in its harness in midair. While some people acted cruelly, others adorned their animals with flower garlands and colorful blankets.

Ugly scenes took their toll, and we engaged in any available activities that offered distractions. There was always a party to attend. One evening, Ernie Richards, a bachelor and the Corps travel agent, invited a few couples to his house. John had taken up the habit of smoking cigars on five-hour flight missions over Korea. Irene Scott smoked cigarettes, and at Ernie's party, she pulled out her pack. "Give me one of those, Irene." In an attempt to discourage John, I lit up and puffed. The first and last cigarette ever to enter my mouth did not faze my husband.

On another occasion, Irene came to our house to bake a cake for a party we were to attend. She finished her stacked-high dessert with iced perfection and stored it in our freezer. By the time we arrived with the cake, the icing ran. Irene was upset. "How long was it out of the freezer before you left to come here?" She blamed me, but we both knew things wilted under Pakistan's heat.

The end of our first year in Karachi approached when I heard of a Baptist mission, and we began attending Sunday services. Missionary Charles Coleman and his wife were from Oklahoma. In-country for a number of years, they had adopted twelve Pakistani children of all ages. I kept contact with this family long after we, and they, had returned to the States.

In November, the Beechcraft reached eight hundred hours of flight time. John and Lieutenant Weiss flew it to Switzerland for a check up and any needed repairs or maintenance. Sergeant Lloyd Haag, the mechanic, went along. The overhaul took weeks. While waiting, John and Lloyd left Lieutenant Weiss, a bit of a loner, and rode the trains into Austria and Germany. Lloyd, stationed in Germany earlier, was able to order ham and fried eggs in German. "Schinken mit spiegeleier." And ask, "Where is the train station? Wo ist der bahnhof?"

On their return flight to Karachi, they encountered waves of foul weather in Italy. The oncoming fronts kept them under unfavorable conditions, and they decided to venture over the mountain range to escape it. The plane's wings and windshield iced up, and they landed in Brindisi, on the east coast of Italy's boot heel. After checking weather conditions, John filed a new flight plan to Athens, Greece. The flight from Brindisi to Athens had them flying over the Mediterranean Sea at night and in a tremendous thunderstorm.

Flying through the rough weather, they sweated over their schedule. At Athens they were relieved to still be on target. Keeping on schedule was critical. Upon landing in Beirut, they had permission to overfly Damascus, Syria, or they would have to initiate a new clearance, requiring thirteen days notice. John had filed to overfly Damascus while still in Switzerland.

Out of Athens and somewhere over the Greek Islands, John noticed oil seeping from the right engine cowling, and the oil pressure showed fluctuation. Shutting down the right engine, they proceeded to Beirut International Airport and landed with one engine. Sergeant Haag inspected the leakage and found recently installed o-rings on the oil by-pass valve to be the wrong size. Wrapping the valve recess with a fine brass wire to make the o-rings fit, Lloyd declared the plane flyable, and the crew took off to overfly Damascus on schedule on the way to Dhahran, Saudi Arabia.

My husband never shared his near mishaps with me. Over the years, I heard bits and pieces as he related his stories to others. Looking back, it was a blessing that I didn't know.

When John returned from Switzerland, we were assigned a different villa.

Colonel and Mrs. DiGiacomo left for stateside, and we moved into their vacated house after living in the PECHS District for a little less than a year. Owned by a diplomat to Spain, the sky blue stucco on the northeastern edge of Karachi in the KDA District, had a healthy dark green grassy front lawn. Flowerbeds held bloomers of many varieties, and bougainvillea draped the compound walls. Concrete covered the back yard. It was a definite improvement over our first quarters.

Although still in a Pakistani neighborhood, we lived within walking distance of other American families.

Without fear, our "babas," as servants referred to children, walked a couple of blocks up the street to play with their friends.

The compound wall was a sidewalk-width from the street, and there was about the same distance between the side of the house and the wall. Johnny and his playmates established a roof floor vantage point from which to throw water-filled balloons onto unsuspecting cart drivers on the street. The boys dropped their ammunition then ducked behind the roof wall until the cart passed.

Lindsey discovered a Pakistani girl enrolled in her American School class lived nearby. They became playmates. A good crop of American boys resided in our neighborhood, but Mary and Sue Scott, and Cheryl Benson were the only girls our daughter's age.

We weren't encouraged to socialize with Pakistanis, and indeed, at times of fanatical Muslim religious rites, we were warned to remain off the streets. One such annual event had male members of the sect walking the streets and beating their backs with chains. We heeded the warnings and never felt threatened during our stint in Pakistan.

President Eisenhower came to Karachi in early December 1959. Pakistanis and Americans gave him a royal welcome. We took our children to the Embassy to hear his speech to the American community. Johnny and Lindsey, along with other children, had seats on the ground right in front of the president. They were barely visible in the next day's newspaper photo. John held Steven and David on his shoulders, but we were too far back in the crowd to make the newspaper picture.

After Eisenhower's speech, we moved to Elephinstone Street. A parade of horse-drawn Victorian carriages conveyed the president, Embassy bigwigs, Pakistani officials and dignitaries past the crowds of common people thronging the sidewalks or hanging from rooftops. A Pakistani friend of Sergeant Haag's invited us to view the parade from his rooftop.

People hung from windows and stood on other roofs to get a glimpse of the U. S. president. Outdoor sweepers ran behind the carriages to sweep up any horse manure.

Christmas came, but holiday carols, color and bright lights were conspicuously absent on the streets of Karachi. We put up a tree, decorated the house and invited some fifty people to sing carols. After the caroling party, I wrote our parents the Christmas spirit finally arrived.

We listened with pride to the school choir as Johnny and Lindsey participated in the Christmas pageant. A stable scene with live sheep, lambs, donkeys and camels portrayed the way it was at the birth of Jesus.

Christmas turned out to be a beautiful and memorable occasion.

Our new year began with an afternoon party hosted by one of the Corps civilian engineers. He provided a variety of entertainment, including elephant rides and an indoor swimming pool. Johnny and Lindsey jumped into the pool before we could think about safety. It turned out in this instance that contaminated water was the least problem. Lindsey couldn't swim, and when she got into difficulty, Johnny grabbed his sister and helped her to the edge of the pool.

In January, Boyce Buckner flew in with John. We tried to rent a bunder boat, but all the boats were reserved for Pakistan's Armed Forces Day celebration. The boat, a single, tall sail, fishing vessel built to trawl in the harbor and near coastal sea, could carry about fifteen people. Another feature was the long board spanning the width of the hull and extending over a good six to eight feet on each side. A crewman sat out over the water on the plank's end to keep the boat from capsizing. When it tipped the other way, he ran to the opposite end to maintain balance.

Americans usually experienced one bunder boat adventure during their stay in Karachi. We had two and wanted to share another with Boyce, but that day, because no boats were available, we hired two Victorian carriages and toured the city.

January and February were cooler months, and we didn't visit the Sandspit beach house. We had an unreliable car problem around that time. Karachi always held a few surprises. City streets weren't easy on automobiles. One night we made our way to a party when John hit a large pothole. The jolt broke the axle on our 1957 Nash Rambler station wagon. The hose from the radiator to the water pump and a nicked fan belt needed replacements. My husband had patched the hose once, but it was beyond patching again. John's dad sent the water hose and fan belt by airmail. The axle was shipped, and the Corps motor pool made the repairs.

By April, the car ran well for John and Johnny's birthdays. Children's birthday parties were big deals. At his '59 party we had gifted Johnny with two parakeets and a cage. I don't think our son was too thrilled with Punch and Judy. Except on occasions when I walked by and stopped to talk to them, or when the hamal cleaned their cage, those were two lonely birds hanging out on the screened porch.

For his 1960 birthday we gave him a bunder boat party. Only boys his age were invited. After the boat ride, all returned to the house for a luncheon, birthday cake, and opening of gifts.

Again, our son didn't seem overly thrilled with the carved model of a sailboat. How was a kid to play with a fully rigged boat when there were no streams? The only flowing water we ever saw was at stinky corner.

By this time, the Buckners had moved from Kharian and lived up the street in the house Joyce Haag recently vacated. With Judy, Paul, and baby Jack, Joyce left Karachi early, for the States. Boyce was to inherit the Beechcraft when we departed Pakistan. Captain John Young was coming to replace Lieutenant Weiss.

The Buckners' dachshund, Sahiba, produced a litter, and at his party, Johnny received a birthday card from Gary and Kevin, stating his gift was a puppy to be given when old enough to leave the mother. When he was six weeks old, they brought the chosen puppy with a large red ribbon about his neck. Our son named him Skipper. He became the family's adored pet.

Skipper's markings were perfection. A shiny black coat enhanced by a rich brown facemask, two brown circles on his chest, and four brown paws. He loved us unconditionally, and developed a means of communicating expression through the dancing brown dots above his eyes.

We already had Rupee, an Alsatian. The Aden family left him with us when they returned to the States. As Skipper grew into a frolicking pup, we took the dogs on walks out toward the cricket field, some distance from the house. Rupee circled us and threatened pie (wild) dogs when they approached. Our dachshund acquired our big dog's bravado. Later it would get him into a lot of trouble for which we paid high-cost veterinarian bills.

In Pakistan, Harvey Aden was a civilian chief engineer. Back in the States, the family lived in Huntsville, Alabama, and he worked with Werner von Braun on rocket projects. A few months after they left for the U. S., we received a letter. "We miss Rupee and have decided we want him with us after all. Would you be willing to give him back to us?"

We crated Rupee and took him to the airport for shipment to Huntsville. Another letter came after the Adens received him. His crate was damaged and Rupee was badly dehydrated, but he recovered.

As are most kids, ours were picky eaters. They didn't care for Khan's egg tarts. David could stir green peas around on his plate long after I demanded, "Sit there until you eat your peas and think about all the kids who have nothing to eat." He always outlasted me. One day, Khan made packaged, dehydrated chicken noodle soup for lunch. None of the four wanted it. When I turned my back, Johnny poured his glass of lemonade into his soup. When I learned what he had done, I told him he would have to eat it. I walked away, and he ran outside and dumped his bowl's contents into the mali pond.

After his birthday, Johnny came down with the Karachi trots and I fired Khan. On our first full day in Karachi, I had told him he would be dismissed if any member of my family became ill from food he prepared. Later, I was told he spent hours at an American friend's home, visiting with her servants. Then, a few pieces of silver tableware turned up missing.

I don't know what happened to the silverware, but I never believed Khan was a thief. Firing him was a big mistake. Johnny soon recovered from the trots. I had allowed a few minor infractions to sway me, and regretted that we didn't sponsor Khan for U. S. citizenship.

Without the cook-bearer, I had to learn to make bread, to buy produce from Empress Market and treat it for consumption, do the cooking, boil water, and help the new hamal, Mohammid, with the laundry. Diliwar (first hamal) and Violet (ayah) were long gone when Khan was dismissed. We never replaced the nursemaid. Mohammid did housekeeping, helped in the kitchen, and served meals. Bashira, the indoor sweeper still kept the floors clean, but we didn't need an outdoor sweeper at the new house. The chowidar-mali pulled guard duty and looked after the garden. We were down to three servants, if I didn't include myself.

Meantime, as I fell into our new routine, John received a letter from the Transportation Corps that he would go to the Advance Transportation Officers Course at Fort Eustis, Virginia, when his Pakistan tour ended.

While we neared the end of our second year in Karachi, all of us needed a change of station. In May 1960, John was given a week of leave for "rest and relaxation." We planned to fly to New Delhi, but my chronic right ear problem acted up, and doctors said I shouldn't fly. I was so ready for any place, having gone no more than fifteen miles to the beach house in over a year. Given treatment at the clinic, I was soon released to fly.

THE TAJ MAHAL IN MOONLIGHT

We landed at the New Delhi airport on a military plane. A man approached us and introduced himself as P. N. Singh. A clean-shaven Sikh, he didn't wear a turban with long hair tucked underneath. He appeared western but for his dark complexion and Asian Indian features.

P. N. offered to drive us downtown to the Hotel Imperial, where we had reservations. He led us to a small sedan similar to a London cab. We were soon on a hairy ride, dodging people, animals, carts and many more automobiles than were seen in Karachi.

Nevertheless, we realized we were in another place very much like Pakistan.

At the hotel, P. N. took the luggage to our second-floor suite then offered to be our guide for the week. We talked about terms, and accepted his offer. "I'll return in the morning to start your tour," he said.

Secure in our arrangements, we settled in and took time to gaze out the windows on the New Delhi skyscape.

After breakfast the next morning, P. N. knocked on the door. He took us through bazaars, which looked no different from those in Karachi, and drove around New Delhi streets before pulling to a stop in front of a jewelry bazaar.

Inside, a walla greeted us with an invitation to sit on benches along the wall. He disappeared for a few minutes and returned with newspaper-wrapped bundles beneath his arms. Opening one bundle with a flourish, his semiprecious gems scattered out onto the wooden floor. We selected a few stones, paid him, and took our leave.

Our next stop was to be the Red Fort, but before we reached it, P. N. glanced down at Steven, seated between him and Johnny. "Ali Baba." He laughed.

Our five-year-old son turned a frown up to him. "I'm not a thief."

From the back seat, I asked, "P. N., why do you think Steven should be called Ali Baba?"

He didn't answer, but glanced at Steve. "What do you have in your pocket, Baba?" Our child looked surprised. Then, P. N. told about our son picking up one of the gems from the bazaar floor and putting it in his pocket.

"Turn around, P. N., we must return it."

"Ah, Memsahib, no need. It's not worth much."

I gave in, and we proceeded on to the Red Fort for an interesting walk through ancient history. A man sat astride a wooden workbench cutting a piece of marble. He pulled a thin wire attached to a bow back and forth like a two-man saw. Every few minutes, he stopped to pour water on the wire. Since he spoke no English, we couldn't ask how long the task took to complete.

Next, across from the fort, we left P. N. standing at the bottom of the stair to the largest mosque in New Delhi. We climbed the wide span of many steps, and almost to the top, encountered two old men deep in conversation. Seeing Steven and David in short pants, both jumped up, unwrapped their dirty, white headgear, and secured it around the boys' lower bodies.

We didn't react, but at the top of the stairs, we removed our shoes and entered a large open space with overhead cover and a highly polished stone floor. It was the place where Muslims answered an Imam's loudspeaker call to face Mecca and pray five times a day.

It was evident that the dirty headgear bothered Steve, known in our family as Mr. Clean. David, on the other hand, cared less about having his legs in a dirty rag. A bit like Pig Pen in the Peanuts comic strip, we could dress David in a suit, and his shirttail would hang out of his pants before we reached the church. His tie would be askew, and sometimes his hands and knees were scrubby from collecting all kinds of objects to store in his pockets. But he was one contented kid.

I never understood those mosque men's need to cover our sons' legs. Lindsey and I wore dresses, showing our legs. Perhaps they were short of headgear. Johnny wore long pants. Had they wrapped his legs, he would have told the old gents he didn't appreciate their dirty rags.

Leaving, we allowed them to remove their headwear, and P. N. returned us to the hotel. He left us to find our own dining experience. Somehow we survived the hotel's unappetizing buffet outlay. We consumed fish, drank papaya and mango cocktails and bottled Coca Colas. Cokes were a no, no in Karachi. Fortunately, we didn't come down with New Delhi trots.

That night, I awoke to find our six-year-old daughter sleep-walking toward a window without glass or screen, and a drop of several floors down. The incident robbed my sleep for the rest of the night.

Over the next two days, P. N. took us to ancient towers, more forts, gardens, and other historical places. Then it was time to make the drive to Agra to see the Taj Mahal.

Driving south of New Delhi we met wedding wagons going to the places of ceremony. "It's the marrying season," P. N. said. Wedding celebrations sometimes lasted a week. Pulled by camels or water buffalos, the brightly painted, floral designed conveyances carried the bride and her family to the event. We passed wagons returning brides and their families to their homes. "If a father betroths his daughter at a tender age, he takes the bride back to his home until she matures and is sent to her husband," P. N. explained. It could be a matter of years.

On toward Agra, we passed through small villages where people stopped to stare at our passing vehicle. Coming upon a man riding an elephant, P. N. pulled off the road and conned him into rides for the kids. Although they had ridden an elephant before, they climbed aboard the huge, ripple-skinned, almost hairless pachyderm and enjoyed another ride.

Arriving at the Taj Mahal compound in mid morning, P. N. dropped us at the gate with instructions to return there when we were ready to leave.

Right away, Johnny spied a water buffalo circling in the distance and ran to investigate. Yoked to a wooden beam, the animal trudged around a well, pulling up water then dumped into a holding vat and used for watering plants, animals, and fowl kept in the compound.

Peacocks captivated Steven and David with their fanned tail plumes, and Lindsey held out nuts and cereal to the monkeys that clustered around her. We had quite a scare when one nipped her hand.

The sprawling gardens offered a profusion of color in plants, trees and blossoms, which my flora-loving husband found most pleasing. Our walk through the gardens took us to the mausoleum sited on a bank of the Yamuna River where it made a bend.

Mogul Emperor Shah Jahanir, meaning King or Lord of the World, had the monument built between 1630-1648 as a symbol of love for his favorite wife, Arjumand Banu Begum.

One of the architects, Ustad Ahmed Lahwari, was born in Lahore, Pakistan, and his Islamic influence on the monument was evident. He also designed the Red Fort in Delhi. I gazed in awe at the stark but delegate beauty of the raised, white marble platform with its grand dome, symmetrically true with surrounding minarets. In front, trees lined the long reflecting pool that divided the gardens. The whole resembled a watercolor painting.

Removing our shoes, we stepped inside onto the black and white marble floor. Gems and semiprecious stones studded the empty, white marble tomb cenotaph honoring Mumtaz Mahal, as the shah's wife was later known. Mosaic inlays of precious stones, such as jade and jasper bursting into floral patterns, adorned the dome and walls of white marble

We viewed a magnificent work of art while some visitors threw flowers onto the vault.

Walking out into the bright sunlight, we had a visitor take our picture on a bench at the end of the reflecting pool with the Taj in the background. It turned out to be out-of-focus, but was the only evidence that we had been there.

Again, we strolled in the lovely gardens. An arched bridge spanned the Yamuna River behind the Taj Mahal, reaching the opposite bank where Shah Jahan had a black marble mausoleum started to memorialize himself. The story was that his family had him declared insane when construction proved too costly. His monument was never completed.

As time drifted into late afternoon, we decided to stay and view the Taj under moonlight. Back at the gate, P. N. came to meet us, and we told him the decision to prolong our stay.

"Sahib, kindly step over here, please?" He took John aside.

In a few minutes, my husband returned. "The police are detaining P. N." He showed the car keys P. N. had shoved into his hand. "He wants me, when we leave the Taj, to drive out to a side road, park, and wait until he can join us." These instructions set my hair on end.

Around nine o'clock in the evening, we sat on a low stonewall, taking in the awe-inspiring moonlit paragon. "What do you think, kids? Is that a pretty sight, or not?"

"It looks like a castle," Lindsey said.

"What are those things on top of the towers?" Johnny asked.

"They're minarets, a signature of Arabic architecture, or the shape a structure is given by the designer."

"It looks like a picture someone painted." Steve already demonstrated his artistic talent.

"John?"

"Yeah, it's pretty."

"Well, next to the Lincoln Memorial in moonlight, I think it is the prettiest thing I've ever seen."

Thrilled with our day, around nine o'clock, we walked back to the gate and rode away in P. N.'s car.

A good distance out, John came to a side road, pulled onto it, and parked to wait. We were tired, and the kids soon fell asleep. I don't know what my husband was thinking, but there in the darkness, thoughts sent shivers up and down my spine. "What if P.N. failed to show up? We don't know the route back to New Delhi. There aren't any vehicles going anywhere."

"Don't worry. He'll be here soon," John said.

Despite his reassurance, I suspected he was concerned, too.

Around midnight, a car pulled up beside us, and P. N. got out. He slipped into the driver's seat, and it was early morning when we arrived back at the Hotel Imperial.

Next day, P. N. took us to a New Delhi temple where Hindus showed respect for their many gods and goddesses by throwing flowers around the statues housed in individual creches.

Buddhists, on the other hand, allowed cows and water buffalos to roam the streets, as they considered all living things to be sacred. Their religion taught that right living, right thinking, and self-denial enabled the soul to reach Nirvana—a divine state of release from pain, sorrow, and desire.

P. N. exposed us to his religion. "Sikhism, is a Hindu sect founded in the north of India around 1500. It adheres to the main principles of belief in one god and rejection of the caste system."

Somehow, I got the impression that P. N. lacked religious fervor. For instance, he probably operated his touring service without a license, and that was cause to detain him back at the Taj.

Nevertheless, he was jovial, and we became attached. He treated us to a trip to the American Embassy in New Delhi and to the Ganges River, a few miles east of the city. We stood on the banks, watching bathers purify themselves in the Holy River. Mother Ganges, revered as a goddess, cleansed the faithful of sins and assisted the dead on the way to heaven. Ashes of cremated bodies were strewn on the Ganges and flowed to the ocean.

We visited the Rajghat, the cremation grounds on the Yamuna River where Mahatma Gandhi was cremated in 1948. On the day we visited, flames consumed five corpses on pyres.

The night before we were to leave India, we witnessed part an elaborate wedding procession. The groom, in gaily-gowned garb, rode on horseback down the street, followed by a large crowd of loud celebrants.

Next day, our week in the "Jewel of Asia," ended. P. N. retrieved our luggage, and us, from the hotel and drove to the airport. We bade him goodbye and boarded an Embassy Flight on a C-54 back to Karachi. For many years after, we kept in touch with P. N., until one Christmas our greeting returned. He was a superb guide who made our week in India exciting and a real learning experience.

SURGERY IN A PAKISTANI HOSPITAL

Rested and relaxed, we returned to Karachi and picked up our lives where we left off.

John flew north on a five-day trip, then he was off on a two-week trip to Dhahran, Saudia Arabia, for his flight physical.

He returned by the time my Cub Scout Den performed a skit I wrote about a pilot landing his plane under instrument readings and control tower directions. Johnny and other scouts acted out the scene before parents and guests on a stage in some building we were allowed to use. The only way to get behind the stage was by way of steps in front of the stage. One little fellow couldn't remember his lines, and was cued from the edge of the platform in front of guests.

In late May, John received a letter regarding a change of assignment. Slated to go to Fort Eustis, Virginia, instead he was selected to attend the U. S. Navy's Test Pilot School at Patuxent Naval Air Test Center in Maryland. He must register at the school by October 1960. This meant we would depart Pakistan after twenty months of his two-year tour.

Given a choice to return to the States by plane or ocean liner, we chose the month-long voyage by liner. John reserved staterooms on two ships, the Italian *Victoria* and Cunard's liner, the *Independence*.

Anticipating travel across the ocean on a big ship was far better than going to summer school, but all four kids entered the first of June.

In August, regular school opened. Johnny began fourth grade, Lindsey second, and Steven started first grade. David went to kindergarten.

About this time, John was up north when one evening I developed a severe headache and vomiting nausea. It was another bout with my ear.

Next day at the Embassy Clinic, two doctors made examinations. "There's something in there. I want you to see a Pakistani doctor who trained at Johns Hopkins and has equipment to detect your inner ear malady." Doctor Winters made an appointment.

Late one evening, John drove me to the doctor's office. He tested my balance, and I failed. Looking in my ear through a high-powered scope, he said, "It appears to be a tumor." He wanted to perform surgery, but clinic doctors suggested penicillin to control infection until I could get back in the States.

I went every two weeks for the shots. One day the nurse broke the needle as she gave the shot in my derriere. Her fingernail scraped across the needle puncture. A carbuncle developed, and it had to be removed.

The day of surgery, John had a flight up north, so Captain Buckner and his driver came early to drop me at the door of Seventh Day Adventist Hospital.

I walked inside with an armful of magazines, and checked in at the reception counter in a long waiting room where wooden benches lined the wall. I was the lone patient in the room. After giving a shot to relax me, the hypo guy said, "Be seated over there." He pointed to a bench.

I sat flipping pages of a magazine when suddenly I felt faint. "Nurse, nurse." My voice sounded feeble as I slipped from the bench.

I came to seconds later. People from the check-in counter were at my side. Someone snatched up and deposited me on a wooden table resembling a large butcher's block in a small side room. A doctor appeared, and soon I was taken to a room with a similar, wooden table.

From that point, I remembered nothing until my eyes opened in a long ward filled with Pakistani patients, all staring at me. I had slept all day, and soon Boyce walked into the ward.

Released to him, I was given a barf bag, and his driver took us home. Bonnie stayed with me that night. I went to the Embassy Clinic for surgical dressings daily.

On the afternoon of August 1st, Steven's birthday party brought scads of Corps kids to eat cake made at the Salateen Club, according to Lindsey's letter to her grandparents.

Several weeks after the surgery, we invited people to our last party before leaving for the States. Our guests insisted that I perform my Indian dance, so I donned my costume. John swore my performance was impressive, but on one of those Russian squats, I braced myself with one hand to keep from sitting on the floor. That wasn't one of the dance moves.

All the Corps officers and their wives attended another party hosted by Madar and other Pakistani drivers in downtown Karachi. We sat on a roof as main courses were served. Then came dessert, ice cream topped with a daub of melted silver. Americans gave each other a glance that asked, "What do I do now?" We ate around the melted silver and listened to conversations between the guys and their drivers.

Madar told about his sister going to a water point. "A man said she couldn't have water. She came and told me. I took a piece of wood to the water point and clubbed the man over the head. Then, sahibs, I filled her water jar."

Our departure time grew closer, and we were given a big going-away party. Saying goodbye to friends always left sadness in my heart.

U. S. Charlie, John and the boys' Pakistani barber, came for their last haircut, as he had every month previously. Whether through him or not, unknown Pakistanis heard by word-of-mouth about our departure. They came eager to buy our pink and white '57 Rambler.

John took the car for an appraisal, and the four-year-old station wagon sold for $2,000. Our Amana freezer, wringer washing machine, and other items were sold as well.

The time came to say goodbye to Mohammid, Bashira and the chowidar, and to send for the Chinese packers. They showed up on

September 8th ready to crate many brass and copper items, tabla drums, camel saddles and cane furniture. When all was packed and boxed, they sent a camel cart to pick up three large shipping crates.

The night of our departure on September 10th, Madar took us to the port. We said goodbye and boarded the *Victoria*, a large Italian ocean liner. Later that evening, Boyce and Bonnie came to the harbor to wish us *bon voyage*.

The kennel was already closed for the night when we came aboard, so Skipper, our four-month-old dachshund, was allowed to stay in the State Room with us. About midnight, the *Victoria* moved out past the harbor breakwater into the open water of the Arabian Sea. We were on our way home.

Our stay in Pakistan was quite a sojourn. Living there was an adventurous experience, a learning time for John and me, and our young children. In the early Sixties, it was much like stepping back into biblical times.

Now, new adventures lay ahead of us. The Arabian Sea crossing and through the Suez Canal; a stopover in Yemen; the Mediterranean Sea; a week in Italy; a boat shuttle into Nice, France; the Strait of Gibraltar; the North Atlantic Ocean-crossing; and finally arriving in New York. But, those adventures were a whole other story.

CROSSING THE ARABIAN SEA INTO THE MEDITERRANEAN

At midnight on September 10, 1960, the *Victoria* pulled out beyond the port of Karachi into the open sea. We went to bed, and I said "goodbye" to Pakistan, thinking it might be nice to revisit someday.

Our first day out, we awakened and gazed through the porthole at sun sparkles dancing on the ocean surface. An almost boundless excitement over the opportunity of such a voyage suddenly calmed when I noticed Johnny atop his bunk, swaying from side to side with the ship's movement. "Look, Mom, we're rocking." He laughed.

Lindsey and I didn't laugh. Nausea struck, and we headed for the bathroom.

Leaving us, John took Skipper and the boys and headed for the kennel, then the dining room. After breakfast, my husband checked on us. "Skipper is one unhappy animal." It was our dachshund's first separation from his family.

About mid-morning, Lindsey and I recovered enough to go for breakfast. Then after exploring the ship, relaxing in deck chairs, and watching sea life, we visited Skipper in the tarp-cordoned deck area outside the kennel. Happy to see us, he demonstrated his hyper-dynamic nature by bouncing from one side of the pen to the other, and yapping himself hoarse.

At dinner that evening, our waiter brought a tray of condiments to our table. For almost two years we had not eaten a raw carrot, celery sticks, and other vegetables. We swooped away every nosh on the platter. The waiter returned, saw the empty tray and laughed. "I'll bring another." It, too, lasted one round of the table. "I know where you boarded," he said.

"You couldn't guess in a million years," I said.

He laughed again. "Karachi. It's the same for all Americans leaving that port." He pampered us with fresh pineapple slices and other delights.

The second day out, we met the Italian kennel keeper on our way to breakfast. Skipper was leashed and being fed on the deck away from the other animals. We stopped to converse, but of course couldn't understand a word he said. Someone came along to interpret. "Your dog was seasick last night," we were told. The keeper laughed, and our interpreter said, "He gets filet mignons while other animals eat fish. He says this one is the youngest animal in the kennel."

We felt Skipper was in good hands, and after breakfast we explored more of the ship with our children.

As voyage days passed, we kept busy with many onboard activities. Our four kids spent hours in the ship's playroom, or enjoyed the swimming pool, costume competitions and tea parties. They competed in their Sindhi suits, chemises of varied-color stripes worn over black sharliwars with round-shaped tribal caps to match. They didn't win the competition, but in my biased opinion, they should have.

As the carbuncle surgery on my bum healed, there were daily visits to the ship's doctor for dressing changes. We practiced the ship's emergency drills for any untoward happening and tried to keep up the children's school lessons. Those necessary events took only a few minutes out of our pleasant days on the sea.

At four o'clock each afternoon, adults were served a high tea. Every evening, John and I enjoyed an Italian songster accompanied by a musical combo. His romantic tunes soothed like a honey body massage, even though we couldn't understand a word of Italian. We kept company with a couple from Cairo, an American wife and Egyptian husband. While she and John talked, the husband and I took to the dance floor. Dancing on a rolling ship wasn't easy but was great fun to try.

On another evening, John and I entered the adult costume competition. He wore a striped, raw silk jacket and gray lamb's wool Jinnah cap. Yes, pants, too. I dressed in a silver *lamé* top and wrapped in a sari of metal gray silk with silver thread woven in floral designs. My outfit was more beautiful than unusual. Like our kids, we didn't win, but it was a fun evening.

I don't recall how many days passed before we reached the port-of-call at Aden, Yemen. We left the ship and traveled inward to the salt fields. Acres and acres of salt water pooled in flat, shallow dugouts, leaving layers of white drying in the otherwise sandy expanse. Aden, at that time, wasn't much of a place. Our visit covered only a few hours.

Back on the ship, we visited with Skipper three or four times each day, enduring his manner of showing happiness for being with his family. He barked loud enough to be heard throughout the ship, and bounded from wall to wall in the tarp enclosure on one end of a deck.

Leaving the Gulf of Aden, the *Victoria* entered the Red Sea with Saudi Arabia on the right and Ethiopia on the left. On past Sudan, we came to the port of Suez, where boatloads of venders met our ship. We weren't allowed to disembark before entering the Suez Canal, unless our intent was to tour the pyramids. Johnny and I voted to visit them, but because camel rides were involved, John and the other three outvoted us. Missing this opportunity was a big regret of my lifetime.

Although missing the pyramids was disappointing, it must not go unnoted that passage through the Suez Canal was interesting in itself. After giving the venders their shot at customers, the ship eased in line behind other vessels and waited its turn through the canal locks. It appeared the large ocean liner would scrape both landsides as it slid through the narrow opening. Slow progress and closeness allowed us to almost reach out and touch people as they went about late afternoon activities.

The ship exited the canal at Port Said and entered the Mediterranean Sea. Back in open waters, we lined the decks to watch waterfowl careen overhead, and soon playful porpoises arced and dived past us. Passing vessels brought us to the deck rails and made us feel we weren't alone in the seemingly wide ocean expanse.

We practiced more emergency drills and tried to keep up the children's school lessons.

All of these events made time speed along. Eight days after departing Karachi, we docked in Naples, Italy and had a wild cab ride to our hotel. We were to be in Italy for five days before boarding the *S. S. Independence*.

BEANS. BUSES AND POMPEII

The first day in Naples, we leashed Skipper and took him on a walk outside our hotel. Our puppy went everywhere with us. In restaurants, his leash looped around table legs while he waited for us to eat. Europeans take a two or three hour rest from noon until around three or four o'clock. The first time we tried to eat at the American lunch hour, closed doors greeted us. Once we caught on, we enjoyed pastas, cannellini (white beans), and fresh salads with olives.

Poor Skipper. At the hotel, he drank water from an ashtray, but on our outings he suffered thirst. I spotted a pet shop. "I'm going to get a water bowl and ask for water."

"How are you going to do that?" John said, knowing I spoke no Italian.

I walked up to the shopkeeper, pointed to Skipper, and cupping hands at my mouth, I lapped like a dog. In two shakes, I had a water bowl and water for our puppy.

Next day, we booked a bus tour of the Amalfi Drive, a loop through southern Italy. On the drive across the boot to the east coast, our family of seven, counting Skipper, filled the long seat across the back of the bus. Soon we were conversing with American school teachers along for the tour. They helped entertain our children, when the Italian guide wasn't leading us in songs or entertaining with operatic arias. He did this without missing one point of interest along the way.

We traveled down the coast on a narrow, mountainous road, careening around curves in which the end of the bus seemed to fly out over the steep cliff. "I'm hanging over the cliff," Johnny yelled, his eyes as large as saucers. The sea lay far below, with vineyards covering arable areas all the way to the water's edge.

Around noon we headed for an eatery on a passageway so narrow a car meeting us could not squeeze by our vehicle. Our driver began backing up so near to the edge that all we could see on the left was water far below. Heavy breathing and loud gasps escaped lips until the bus reached a point that allowed the car to pass.

After lunch, we circled back toward the west coast and soon neared Mount Vesuvius, elevation four thousand one hundred ninety feet. The mountain erupted in 79 AD, covering Pompeii with ash. For me, Pompeii was the highlight of our tour in Italy. Archeological digs revealed an unbelievable society.

We walked among the excavations began in 1748. A once thriving seaport and spa city was uncovered, revealing an opulent lifestyle of some twenty thousand people. Once a beautiful city, roomy, colonnaded, stucco homes with indoor baths were supplied with water from a gravity-fed system of pipes that ran alongside the streets. Walls were decorated with beautiful, and in some cases, erotic frescoes. At one such place, women and children in our tour group weren't allowed to view the erotica.

Hard crusted streets held chariot ruts from an ancient time.

The volcanic ash preserved forms of human and animal remains, some expressing their horror, and some appearing to pray as they were encased in the ashes. A treasure trove of utensils and household items gave clues into their daily lives. Metal and marble artifacts, such as medical and dental tools similar to some used today, withstood the heat.

Pompeii left me with a yearning to return to that place of antiquity at some future time. A time after continuing excavations revealed more of the city. Back on the Amalfi tour, we stopped at fishing villages and other sites. On the last leg of the drive, we stopped in a village where cameos were made.

After a full day of bus riding and sightseeing, we returned to the hotel. I held Skipper's leash and waited for John to get our room key from the desk near the dining room door. Glancing at our puppy, I saw he had left a pile right in the path of diners. Snatching the key from my husband, I dragged the dog along and hurried ahead to our room. With Kleenex and a wet towel, I ran back downstairs to collect and mop as people circumvented me with expressions of amusement and curiosity.

That evening, we took in Naples nightlife. People milled or strolled leisurely, chatting, laughing and enjoying each other at an hour when Americans would be rushing to get home. I got the impression that Italians were a happy people.

Colorful city lights reflected on softly lapping Mediterranean waters, a scene of Napoli still vivid in my memory.

The next day, we boarded a train to Rome.

A ROMAN HOLIDAY

We planned two days in Rome, then take the train to Florence and on to Genoa, where we would board the *S. S. Independence* or its sister ship, the *S. S. Constitution*, depending on which was in port. One or the other would transport us for the remainder of our homeward journey.

It was afternoon when the taxi dropped us at the train station in Naples. John purchased tickets. "Is a ticket required for our dog?"

The ticket agent shook his head.

We boarded and found our place in the railcar. Shortly, the train was underway. Interesting scenes zipped past the window. Ancient villages perched atop high hillcrests, and graceful bridges spanned deep gorges. I marveled at the beauty and history of the peninsula shaped like a boot, then a mountain tunnel blotted out light.

We arrived in Rome in late afternoon to be met at the station by a handsome young man of college age. He loaded our baggage and drove us to the hotel, promising to return the next morning to tour us around the Eternal City.

True to his word, he arrived on time and took us downtown. We walked up and down several streets running alongside a shaded park. People strolled to and fro as we peered into shop windows and watched pushcart vendors hawk their wares. A people-watcher by nature, I wanted to remain on a park bench and absorb the images of their dress, their walks, and what I perceived their attitudes to be. But, the day moved along and there were other things to see.

Our guide drove to the Fountain of Trevi. We pitched our coins in the pool and made our wishes. "Mom, I wished for a baby sister." Every birthday Lindsey wished for a baby sister.

At a place offering a view of an ancient aqueduct, we marveled at the stone structure spanning long spaces at treetop level, strengthened only by arched design between stone piers.

Our next stop was the Coliseum. Inside the historic ruin, we walked along one of the tiers and gazed down into the arena. *Quo Vidas*, a 1951 movie with roaring lions, moans and cries of innocent people, clashes of gladiator swords and crowds shouting approval, came to mind. Gazing on a place of ancient Roman mind-set, I found the experience stressful.

That evening, we happened upon the American Restaurant. Thinking the name of the eatery meant American food, we secured Skipper to a table leg and ordered hamburgers. I had a gnawing crave since day one in Pakistan for a good hamburger. The kids seemed to savor their burgers, as though they were in a Howard Johnson's, their favorite stateside eatery. But it didn't fill my expectation of a good old hamburger, hot off the backyard grill.

Next day our energy was restored, and our young guide took us to Vatican City in the morning and the catacombs on the Appian Way in the afternoon.

The Vatican rested on one of the seven hills of ancient Rome and on the west bank of the Tiber River. The September morning was pleasant, and our guide parked the car just off St. Peter's Square. We walked onto the brick-laid plaza where Bernini's 1667 colonnades enfolded the centerpiece—a thirteenth century BC Egyptian obelisk.

Caius Caligula, a Roman emperor, brought the obelisk to Rome from Heliopolis, Egypt, and had it erected in his mother's gardens in 37 AD. We read from a tourist brochure that the present Church of St. Peter rested upon the site of Agrippina's gardens.

Gazing upon the square's covered Iconic-style colonnades with Doric columns, I said, "They reach out as though drawing one into their arms." Bernini's one hundred forty marble statues of saints rose atop the colonnades. Awestruck by the spectacular approach to the architectural beauty of the domed Basilica, my attention turned to the uniformed Swiss guard marching past the bronze entrances.

When he was beyond us, our guide said, "You can enter St. Peter's Church now." So far that morning, we were the only visitors, with the exception of Skipper who trooped along on his leash.

Inside, Michelangelo's dome rose overhead to a great height. Actually, he died before its completion, the brochure stated, and Giacomo, an architect, redesigned it, maintaining many of the artist's plans. The dome was completed in 1560.

After viewing many artistic offerings, we returned to an exit and came upon yet another one of Michelangelo's creations. *Pieta.* Despite the inspiring beauty of Mary's expression of acceptance, gazing down on the sacrificed body of her son draped across her lap, it didn't ring true of a mother to me.

The Sistine Chapel held more of Michelangelo's work. The *Creation of Adam*, one of nine Genesis stories represented on the chapel ceiling, and the artist's version of *The Last Judgment was* located on a chapel wall, as I recall.

The history and artistic talent found in Vatican City boggled my mind, and we still had the catacombs to visit.

Some forty Jewish and Christian catacombs were located around Rome. We were taken to one on the Appian Way, a thoroughfare begun in 312 B.C. and when finished, stretched from Rome to Brindisi as a busy trade road. The Appian Way was said to be the escape route Peter took when he saw a vision of Jesus and turned back to Rome.

At the catacomb site, we descended seven stories to a subterranean burial labyrinth of narrow galleries and small chambers. Walls held chiseled, horizontal recesses the length and depth of a body and stacked tier upon tier to the ceiling. "It's amazing. We're standing among the burial places of early Christians. Kids, someday you must revisit these places."

Our children were too young to understand what they were seeing from a historical perspective, and Skipper couldn't give his dog's view. But I stored feelings and scenes of the Vatican, the catacombs and Coliseum in my memory bank of unforgettable experiences.

Our Roman holiday ended. John inquired about rail tickets to Genoa by way of Florence. That leg of our plans wasn't to be. A devastating flood, notable for ruining artwork in Florence museums, had washed out the rail lines to Genoa. We boarded the train back to Naples, and minutes before arriving at the station, a conductor walked through our car. Skipper slept beside John. He woke, stood up and shook himself, stopping the conductor dead in his tracks. "Ticket for the dog?"

"We were told he didn't require a ticket."

He didn't accept John's explanation and insisted on payment. Pulling out Italian lire, my husband handed him the requested amount, and the conductor stuck the bills in his pocket.

We had one more day in Naples before boarding the ship for the Atlantic crossing.

THE ATLANTIC CROSSING
TO OUR HOMELAND

From Naples we boarded the *Independence* and cruised overnight to Genoa. Next morning we left the ship for the offered cemetery tour.

Our guide pointed out that Christopher Columbus was buried in Staglieno Cemetery, noted for sculptural and architectural monuments to famous people. Some of the explorer's bones and ashes perhaps, but I read later that his remains were in several locations. The primary burial spot of Columbus was in Spain's Cathedral of Seville. Records show some of his remains were in Genoa, and some in Santo Domingo, Dominican Republic.

Located on a hillside, it was difficult to maneuver among the graves, neoclassical porticos and Gothic chapels. Graphic scenes were carved in niches of decaying walls. Sensual statues of marble angels, standing, sitting or reclining, reflected an Italian flair for passionate art and an esthetic approach to honoring the dead. Our guide explained that some graves contained more than one body. A deceased family member might be buried on top of a previously departed to conserve space. Some graves, the guide said, were stacked with more than two corpses.

Limited time allowed us to see only a small portion of the burial site. Back at the pier, we re-boarded and steamed out in late afternoon.

Most of the ship's passengers were Jewish and Italian Americans returning home from holiday in their native lands.

Next morning the *Independence* anchored off the coast of France. John and I left the kids with playroom attendants and took the shuttle boat into Nice. For a couple of hours we walked the streets, peered into shops and bought French chocolates.

Back aboard, we toured our huge floating home, home at least for the next two weeks.

Johnny discovered one of his American schoolmates in Pakistan was on the ship. The two boys roamed all parts of the vessel, wherever they were allowed. Since it was the school season, there weren't many children aboard the *Independence*. No activities were planned for them, so our kids enjoyed swimming and the playroom.

Sometime that night, we slipped through the Strait of Gibraltar and out into the open Atlantic. Ocean waters cooled in the latter part of September, a different experience than the warm Mediterranean in mid-month. Decks were weathered-in with tarps during rainstorms.

As we sailed past the Azores, a retired professor spoke about the islands' history and culture. Beyond the islands, no other land and little else remained to be seen on the crossing.

During the day, John and I took dance lessons from a graceful blonde and her skilled dark-haired partner. They failed to turn us into cha-cha-cha steppers, but at night they entertained on the dance floor with ballroom movements, some slow and romantic, others fast and swirling. We visited the library and sat for hours, relaxing in deck chairs. People on the Italian *Victoria* had been friendlier. The *Independence* presented a more formal setting.

On the twelfth day, John woke us about five o'clock in the morning. "Come here." He called from the porthole. "See the Statue of Liberty." We held the kids up to see the lady with the freedom torch welcoming us into New York Harbor. From the pier, a taxi delivered our dog, luggage and us, with enough clothing to last six people for a month, to our hotel.

Back on American soil, the kids reacquainted themselves with elevators and television.

Skipper, happy to be out of the ship's kennel, ran around the room sniffing and wagging his tail.

As for me, I thought about how different life would be from the last two years. How blessed we were to live in a country that practiced promised freedoms. In a country with regulations about food, water and health care. A place with far less poverty than Pakistan. Again I would face the grind of housework, but that was a minor concern compared to the joy I felt about being back in our homeland.

John picked up a newspaper from the hotel desk, and we searched automobile ads.

That evening we went down on the street to find a local place to have dinner. We wound up in an Automat, a new experience for us. We had trouble locating the money slot and selecting sandwiches and drinks. One lone man watched with a sneering smile on his face. "Can you help us," I asked.

He exhibited the stereotypical reputation of a New Yorker at the time, terse and abrasive, with an air of, "Where are you hicks from?"

I didn't tell him we just arrived from Pakistan, and we hicks were from Arkansas.

The next day, we purchased a 1961 Plymouth station wagon, a green Valiant. Loaded with our baggage, we left New York City in the new car the following day.

A sun-kissed October lay across our travel miles, showcasing brilliant fall colors the likes of which we had not seen in two years. We drove through the countryside, knowing there would be no sheep, cows, camels, and elephants, no bicycles, rickshaws and hordes of pedestrians requiring our attention. No filth and little poverty to gaze upon. Only the beauty of our America. Gosh, it felt good to be home, but we had miles yet to go.

That evening, we arrived in Lexington Park, Maryland, and found a motel. The kids hadn't been confined in the car on extended trips in a long time. Freed that evening, they acted like animals released from a cage. Skipper joined them as they jumped on the beds as though they were trampolines. Then our dog had the shock of being left along while we had dinner. In his dog's mind, he must have thought, What happened? As Skipper Foster I've always tagged along with my family.

Next day, John registered at the Patuxent River Naval Air Test Center's Test Pilot School. He let Commander Leo Krupp know we were going to Arkansas, and he would return to start school on 27th of October.

We expected to live in Lexington Park, located just outside the military gate, for the nine-month duration of the school. When John returned from the base, we went to a rental office and reserved a house in a development built during World War II for navy personnel. The gray two-story, three-bedroom, one-bath domicile sat on the Cabot Place cul de sac, a quiet safe street for our children. Built like a modified Cape Cod without cover over the front door, we called it a "cracker box."

Relieved to have a home to return to, we located the school Johnny, Lindsey and Steven would attend, and drove down the town's only thoroughfare and several branching streets. A number of churches, King's Drugstore, two service stations, a supermarket, movie theater, Rue's Roost—the only watering hole and restaurant—and an antique barn. "It's more than we were accustomed to in the last two years," John said.

Satisfied, we returned to the motel, called my parents and packed to leave the next day.

Chill permeated the morning air when we left the motel. We didn't have fall clothing, but the car's heater kept us comfortable as we headed south to Arkansas for family reunions.

Over the two-week stay, we tried to bring Johnny, Lindsey and Steve up to speed in school lessons. Our families reintroduced us to home-style American food, and we renewed old friendships. Then, like so many times before, we were off to start a new tour in another place.

Back in the car, we took the return two-day trip to Maryland.

LEARNING FROM THE NAVY TO BE A TEST PILOT

John entered Test Pilot School on a chilly day in late October 1960. Class 28 had sixteen members: ten navy men, two marines, one army (John), one Canadian navy, and two civilian engineers. John, the Canadian and two civilians were termed the "cats and dogs" of the class.

Classes were barely underway when someone at the school handed a letter to him. The return address was that of the Chinese packers in Pakistan. The letter stated the camel backed the cart close to the end of the dock, and dumped one of our crates into the water between the ship and pier. It took twenty minutes to lift it out of the drink. They unpacked our goods and spread them over rocks, and the ground to dry. Photos enclosed in the letter didn't reveal the pitted—from salt water—and tarnished condition of silver services and brass pieces. I cried about the ruined family picture albums. "Why did we take our pictures over there? I suppose I thought rats may gnaw on them if we left them in storage."

"Maybe they would have," John said.

Overcoming the shock of losing the pictures, we went about settling into our new home with the purchase of a portable dishwasher and new furniture. The old wrought iron set went into the basement. Our three boys shared a bedroom, using the bunk beds and a twin bed. Lindsey's tiny bedroom had a built up, box-like structure covering something that remained a mystery. The structure ran the length of the inside wall, just right to hold a twin mattress that became her bed.

Johnny, Lindsey and Steven entered Lexington Park Elementary and right away liked their teachers and principal, Mr. Symasko. "He stands in the hall and greets us every morning," Lindsey said. "He visits our classroom, and sometimes he leaves his paddle. We can't take our eyes off it. We are afraid he will come back and use it. He's funny, too. I had a pencil in my mouth. He stopped me and said take it out because it made me look like a native in the jungle."

As his brother Johnny had, David missed out on kindergarten. Classes filled before we arrived in October. John and our school-aged kids geared down to schoolwork, and again I took up the expectations of a military wife, mother, hostess, social bee, and volunteer.

After living in Pakistan, I viewed southern Maryland as paradise. The naval air station snuggled between points where the Patuxent and Potomac rivers emptied into the Chesapeake Bay. It was a region of beautiful land and seascapes, rich in culture and colonial history. Nearby was St. Mary's City, a misnomer. The village consisted of the 1700s State House, an Episcopal church and cemetery, few houses, and St. Mary's College. It was the site of the first permanent settlement in Colonial Maryland. Lord Baltimore came with the Catholics on the *Ark* and *Dove* in 1634, bringing their concept of religious tolerance.

But paradise aside, we lived at the end of the line. Marlow Heights, eighty miles northwest, was the nearest shopping center of any size. Outside the main gate and across a highway, the small village of Lexington Park stretched a distance of about a mile. Small businesses lined its one main street. Since I'm a necessity shopper, driving the distance wasn't a problem for me.

The naval station had a commissary, Post Exchange, service station and a hospital. Writing checks at the commissary and Post Exchange was fun. Our checks carried John's rank of captain. A navy captain ranks evenly with an army full colonel. When captain was noticed on my checks, I zipped right through cashier lines and received fast bagging and courteous loading of groceries into the car. I never owned up to being an army captain's wife.

We were off to a good start, and I didn't suspect the burden nine months of Test Pilot School would place on John and the rest of us. He attended full-day classes on base, came home, had dinner, hit the books, and wrote reports until one or two in the morning. He studied on weekends, as well. The kids were outdoors much of the time, but when in the house, they couldn't disturb him. My husband might as well have been TDY, and the children had a father present in body only. Thinking back, they may not have been affected as much as I imagined, since it was normal for their father to be absent frequently.

While we were all under the strain, I realized John engaged in an unusual assignment. However, I didn't suspect we were socializing with future outstanding achievers. Much later I learned John Glenn and other astronauts had graduated from earlier TPS classes. We were genuinely fond of the TPS commander, Leo Krupp, and his wife. Upon retirement, Commander Krupp became a NASA media consultant and broadcast with Walter Cronkite when a space vehicle launched. Charles "Pete" Conrad, a TPS flight and performance instructor, became an astronaut after we left the navy. A fun kind of guy, Pete was seen on TV during the second lunar landing, hitting golf balls and leaping about on the moon's surface.

We found our friends pleasant and entertaining, but Skipper didn't appreciate his animal visitors. Our puppy developed braveness from watching Rupee ward off wild dogs in Pakistan. He attacked two German Shepherds. Standing beneath Shepherd bellies, he gnawed until one of the bigger dogs took off part of his ear. His first visit to the vet—there would be many more—left his ear stitched, his head in bandages, and our wallet lighter.

Our dachshund had a hard time adjusting to stateside life. I'm not sure he ever did adjust. In his five-month lifetime, he had traversed the Arabian and Mediterranean Seas with us, toured the Amalfi Drive and Pompei in southern Italy, ridden a train to Rome, toured the Eternal City, Colosseum and Roman Catacombs. I think he may have had an

"I am special" complex. He had ways of showing great dissatisfaction when we left him alone.

Many times we returned home to find a toilet-tissued living and dining room. Skipper knew that game long before homeowners awoke to find trees and shrubs gift-wrapped. Taking the end of the roll from the upstairs bath, he pulled tissue down the stairs and strewed it over floor and furniture. We thought to solve the problem by closing the bathroom door, then, he plucked Kleenex from the box and created snowy puffs over the area. We hid the Kleenex box, and he knocked lamps from living room end tables.

If our dog was unhappy when alone, he didn't miss a day of the fun, when just before Thanksgiving two feet of soft fluffy snow fell. He buried up to his belly, but he was right out there on the long slope behind our house with the neighborhood kids on their sleds. Every day as long as the snow lasted, they gathered with their speedy gliders. Our kids and dog spent a fun holiday, plus snow-free days from school.

Unfortunately, Skipper was alone a lot, and David was carted to the base nursery. "Widows" of TPS students formed a social group, and were also members of the larger Navy Officers' Wives Club. There were teas and luncheons to attend. I was no longer in Pakistan, where Khan, and later Mohammid, kept the kids when we went out.

While military wives were encouraged to participate in social activities, I enjoyed being home. Back in the land of television, I watched Senator John F. Kennedy debate Richard Nixon and was captivated by young Kennedy's intelligence and charm. After two years' absence, I had much catching up to do. Washington television stations and *The Washington Post* provided ways for educating oneself. It was a time when TV news was factual rather than opinionated, and the *Post* carried in-depth stories by the likes of Hal Johnston, David Broder, Jules Witcover and other trusted journalists. Excitement ran high when JFK won the presidency. His inauguration, on a snowbound January day, left me feeling we were in good hands.

With John and the kids settled in school, I consulted a navy doctor about my ear surgery. He made an appointment at Bethesda Medical Center. Given a surgery date in February, I was told, "Ear surgery is relatively new. You need a procedure performed by only a few surgeons, but your doctor is the best." The corpsman added, "He's Jackie Kennedy's ENT specialist."

A piece of vein taken from the ankle area was used to reconstruct an eardrum, and my middle ear bones were rebuilt. Upon waking from the anesthetic, I vomited for a night and day until given something to control it. With my head swathed in bandages, I was unaware that hair was shaven from the right side. During the week of hospitalization, I had no visitors. I don't know how John managed during the hospital stay and weeks following, but he did. He cooked meals, took David to the nursery, saw to all the kids needs when he returned from classes, and studied past midnight.

The removal of the tumor was successful, and after healing, a hearing test revealed only thirty-five percent audibility in the ear. Later, the doctor returned to my ear in an attempt to improve hearing, but his try wasn't successful.

Around this time we received a letter from Pakistan. Doctor Winters moved his beautiful red-haired wife and three-year-old daughter into our former villa. His little girl, the letter stated, got into his medical bag, took medication and died.

With surgery and bad news behind us, I helped with school field trips and PTA activities. On one field exploration with Johnny's class, we dug for fossils along the banks of the Chesapeake Bay. As homeroom mother for the second grade, I visited Lindsey's class one day. The teacher asked a question, and my daughter, eager to impress me, held up her hand and was called on. Her answer was wrong. She was embarrassed.

I'm not sure I had ever told her of a similar embarrassment. When my fifth grade teacher, Mrs. Minnie Renick, asked what the President's house was called, I raised my hand and said with great confidence, "It's the United States Capitol." Of course, my classmates laughed, and one answered correctly that it was the White House. After that error, I was reluctant to answer questions in class.

When I wasn't volunteering, I might be at a luncheon meeting in the quaint fishing village on Solomon's Island, or historic Sotterly House, or the Officers' Club facing the Chesapeake. Then, there were outings to keep the kids from disturbing John.

On a summer Saturday, we started out to Glen Echo Amusement Park in Bethesda. Headed out Washington's Wisconsin Avenue, I determined we couldn't possibly have any time at the park and make it back to Lexington Park for their afternoon dental appointments. Imagine the howls when I turned around and headed south again. We never did get to that amusement park, that day or any other.

Some things had to wait until John graduated from TPS. In June 1961 at the graduation ceremony, Admiral Ramsey, commander of the Naval Air Test Center, recognized John as the first Army pilot to complete the navy test pilot school. Ready to let their hair down, the graduates entertained at their ceremony with various performances. John's group of four bared their bellies with painted eyes, noses and lips, to belly sync while whistling the prisoners' tune in the movie, *The Bridge Over the River Kwai*.

Wives celebrated the graduation as much, if not more, than their husbands. Jann Yamnicky wrote a poem, and read it at the ceremony. The poem told the story from the perspective of TPS wives. [Later, Jann's husband, John, was commander of TPS. Unfortunately, he was a passenger on the plane that crashed into the Pentagon on September 11, 2001.]

The graduation ceremony brought an end to a painful nine-month period. Families survived TPS with a welcomed sense of freedom. So did the guys. Several days following their graduation, Class 28 left on a week-long school trip to airplane manufacturing plants—Gruman in Bridgeport, Connecticut, Consolidated Aircraft in Fort Worth, and Boeing on the West Coast.

John returned from the school trip to learn he was assigned to the naval base's helicopter testing facility. We were to be with the navy for another two years.

He took two weeks of leave time, and we started on a trip to Arkansas to visit our families. On the drive south into North Carolina, we stopped the first night west of Asheville in Maggie Valley. The next morning, John took the kids on the twenty-minute chairlift, 4,000 feet up Buck Mountain to the Ghost Town in the Sky. They enjoyed the Wild West, live-action shootout while Skipper and I remained in the motel next to a mountain stream.

Leaving Maggie Valley, we drove through the Cherokee Indian Reservation. Indians dressed in full-feathered attire sat in front of craft shops. On through the Smoky Mountains, we landed next in Chattanooga, Tennessee. After years of seeing barn roof signs across the South stating, "See Rock City," we drove up Lookout Mountain. I don't recall seeing Ruby Falls and Rock City must not have impressed me. But we stood at Lovers' Leap and tried to distinguish the seven states supposedly viewable from that height.

Since I couldn't mark the states in my view, I read the tragic story of Lovers' Leap. The tale goes that an Indian brave named Sautee fell in love with Nacoochee, a Cherokee. Their tribes warred, so the lovers ran away together. When they were discovered, Sautee jumped from Lovers' Leap, and Nacoochee, heartbroken, jumped after him.

We had left the fated couple behind when we noticed Steven was feverish. All four kids had recovered from chicken pox and measles, and Johnny and Lindsey from the mumps. Now, Steve had the mumps. He always ran the highest temperatures, and seemed to suffer most from colds, sore throats, and earaches. Although he swelled up like a puffed toad after we arrived, he behaved like a real trooper, even fishing and visiting Arkansas places of interest with my brother and his wife.

His courage reminded me of the day I stood outside the latched half-door of a lab room, watching a tech stick Steve's arm numerous times in an effort to find a vein from which to draw blood. A single tear ran down my small son's cheek, but he hadn't uttered a sound.

The Foster grandparents liked to fish at a lake on their property. Johnny and Lindsey were in a john boat with their dad when Skipper jumped into the water and began swimming toward them. His short little legs were almost beyond paddling, and I stood on the bank screaming, "He's going to drown," as they rowed to his rescue. Our little dachshund seemed undaunted. His name should have been Trouble, but Johnny insisted on Skipper.

He may have been trouble, but we loved the seventh member of our family, even though it was doubtful my mother did after her exasperating experience with our "wiener" dog. We left him in her care to visit friends, and she accidentally let him get out the door. Skipper took off on our trail with my frantic mother in the car, in hot pursuit. She looked exhausted when she related how she caught him.

At the time, my brother Frank and his wife, Naomi, lived in Rowland, Oklahoma, just across the Arkansas River from Fort Smith. They took us to Petit Jean Mountain in the Ozarks.

Steven healed from the mumps soon after our mountain-touring vacation ended, and back in Maryland, David came down with the communicable disease. He recovered, and we moved into another "cracker box" with a finished basement. Our eldest, Johnny, needed a room of his own. The Cape Cod-like cottage on Essex Drive had yellow siding. Otherwise, it duplicated the gray-sided house on Cabot Place.

With this move, our kids didn't have to face the uneasiness of making new friends. They already knew the neighborhood children as schoolmates.

John reported to the helicopter test facility, and soon we were involved with a whole new group of people. Most members of the VSTOL (vertical, short takeoff and landing) Branch of the Flight Test Division were civilian engineers. Sounding pleased with his new assignment, my husband said, "The enlisted men look out for me."

One of John's first duties was an in-flight performance test of the UH1 Marine helicopter. Manufactured by Bell Helicopter in Fort Worth, our friend, David Gray came from the Bell plant to Patuxent to set up test instrumentation in the UH1. Ruth, Jimmy, and four-year-old Karen came with him, and we took them to Washington sites, including Arlington National Cemetery.

As we walked up to the Tomb of the Unknown Soldier, Ruth thought she had Karen by the hand, but suddenly we heard, "Halt!" Karen had darted under the chain-linked enclosure, and the guard stood with lowered rifle, ready to defend the tomb. "Parents are responsible for keeping children outside the barrier," he shouted.

Ruth enticed Karen out, and caught her hand. As we walked away down the sidewalk, Ruth's face skewed into animated shock. "I do believe he would have shot her."

John was in Philadelphia on the Chinook helicopter test project when word came of his promotion to major. His navy "plane captain" (mechanic), Gunnery Sergeant Snuffy Smith, flew to Philly to present his order of promotion and to pin a gold leaf on John's flight suit.

Whether or not my husband was home, we attended Lexington Park Baptist Church and Sunday School. Johnny and Lindsey were in the Junior Choir. I taught Sunday School and helped with summer Bible School.

Our minister's wife, Mrs. Chapman, and the Cheuvronts' (from TPS Class 28) son took art lessons from Peter Eagley at the church. I was told Peter was from a family of Washington artists known for painting portraits of Supreme Court justices. From an early age, our Steve showed artistic talent, and I enrolled him in Peter's class. Later, I engaged Mrs. Chapman to do a portrait of Lindsey in her red velvet Christmas dress. She entered the finished, life-sized pastel of our daughter in an art competition at St. Mary's College. It won first place in portraits.

Summer turned into a fun time for the kids. A wooded area behind houses across the street was ideal for fort building. Lindsey had a sleep-over which turned into a sleepless party of giggling girls blanketed and pillowed all over the living room floor.

All four of our kids got into big trouble when they went off one evening to play at the Little League ballpark without telling us where they were going. Dinnertime came and they weren't home. John and

I walked the neighborhood calling. I felt panicky, and when we found them, they took a tongue-lashing and were grounded.

If they did chores, the kids earned allowances of twenty-five cents per week. On Saturdays, they walked to the movie theater with quarters in their hot little hands. One Saturday afternoon, our next door neighbor saw them on the sidewalk, heading homeward. He stopped. "You want a ride?"

"No, sir," Lindsey said. "Mom told us, 'Never get in the car with anyone.'"

Our daughter wasn't overjoyed when I happened upon a beautiful antique piano and engaged Mrs. Martin, the church organist and music teacher, to give her lessons. Lindsey practiced with little enthusiasm, and the drive to St. Mary's City for lessons shortened her treasured playtime.

She liked being a Brownie Scout. Slated for a three-day camp-out near the St. Mary's River, I was asked to help her troop leaders. John was TDY, and I agreed to help if the three boys and Skipper could go along. With the exception of a church-organized week in a clubhouse on the Red River when I was around ten years old, I had never camped.

Over the two camp nights, Lindsey shared a tent with several other Brownies while Skipper, the boys and I had our own. At all hours of the night, little girls found trips to the latrine as excuses to use their flashlights. They giggled past our tent, and Skipper barked, and barked. I lay awake, listening to him and waiting for a snake or some other critter to invite itself into our lodging. I guessed no one slept those two nights, and I learned camping wasn't for me. The boys had a camp-out blast. With adult supervision, they built a bridge over a stream.

John helped with Johnny's Cub Scout camp-outs and encouraged him in building his car for the derby race competition.

All of us rooted for him at our eldest son's Little League games.

While the kids had summer fun, Skipper showed a dislike for our postman. Hearing loud shouts one day, I investigated from the front door. Our dog nipped at the mailman's heels. The man delivered a strong kick that only strained Skipper's preexisting negative notions. I ran out and picked up our puppy. "Please, don't kick him. If you stop walking, call him Skipper and let him sniff as you talk to him, he will not try to bite." The postman complied. When he came to the house to tune Lindsey's piano, he and Skipper were already good friends.

Before summer ended, we bought two large wooded lots "as an investment" of $600 each in Placid Bay Estates on Virginia's northern neck. The development, at Maddox Creek's entry into the Potomac, lay ten miles from "Wakefield," George Washington's birthplace, and fifteen miles from "Stratford Hall," the birthplace of Robert E. Lee. The location sounded impressive, and we thought the building sites would be easy sells when we were ready.

On most weekends, we drove sixty miles to Placid Bay. Laboring like Trojans, we cleared underbrush, a good way to spend family time. Skipper enjoyed the outings, and our kids liked fishing and swimming better than the work.

One Saturday, John and Johnny fished across the pond. Lindsey swam, and Steve and David paddled around in plastic rings. I watched them from the bank, when suddenly, I saw Steve disappear beneath the water and his empty ring float away.

Knowing I sank like a rock in water, I screamed, "John, Steve is drowning."

My husband dived fully clothed and in combat boots, wallet in his pocket and watch on his wrist, to pull our child to safety.

Johnny and Lindsey had taken Red Cross swim lessons the previous summer. Classes at the Officers' Club pool filled quickly, but Steve and David awaited their class to begin. Steve's near-drowning incident left him frightened of water. He took the lessons, but he had to repeat them the following summer to overcome his fear.

Summer ended, and David entered first grade. Johnny was a fifth grader, Lindsey in third and Steve second. With all four in school, I felt a certain sense of freedom, but I still had Skipper, the fifth kid. The day he escaped without me on the other end of his leash, I walked up and down, calling. Already late for the wives' club tea at Sotterley House, I drove away from the curb, and there he came, trotting down the sidewalk, two blocks from the house. I stopped the car and let him in. Happy to see me, he jumped from front to backseat to front again, yelping and spreading dirty dog odor. Apparently, he ran with a pack of smelly dogs. By the time I arrived for the tea, I smelled like I had been running with the pack.

There seemed no end to what our dachshund would do. On another day, I went to the base to pick up John. Skipper's ears flapped in the breeze as he leaned into the station wagon's open window. Leaving the base, we approached a service station on the right. Turning my head toward the station, I saw Skipper galloping straight for a man walking toward the street.

"Ye gads! Stop the car, John. Skipper just knocked a man to the ground."

We jumped out and ran to the man as he rose from the pavement and brushed himself off. "Are you injured?" I asked as John picked up our errant dog. The words, "law suit," ran across my brain, and I was sure my husband expected such as well.

The old gent laughed and assured us he wasn't harmed.

Relieved that our lovable, trouble-making dog hadn't put us in court, we went about life as usual. I graduated from Red Cross classes as a Gray Lady, and volunteered at the base hospital one day a week. Dressed in my gray-white stripped uniform, fashioned after a registered nurse's, a matching cap and white oxfords, no jewelry, no perfume, I made ready examining rooms and stayed with the doctor during examinations if the patient was female.

If I wasn't volunteering, I might be sewing. My machine had been used little after the late night stitching bouts when John was in Korea. A lady in Lexington Park offered classes in the Bishop Method of Sewing. I took the lessons and began turning out couture, for Lindsey and me, using Vogue patterns.

Sewing was the least of my concerns in October 1962. President

Kennedy's administration presented photographs of Russian missiles on the island of Cuba. As our blockade confrontation with Khrushchev grew into fear of a nuclear war, we were told to stock food and water, but never where to seek shelter. The crisis was resolved when the Russian leader backed down and agreed to remove the missiles.

The threat of war cooled and sewing was a good pastime when winter dumped yet another deep snow. Under the sun, it thawed a bit then froze at night. We had no electricity for two weeks. John pulled his grill behind the kitchen storm door to cook hamburgers and warm Pork 'n' Beans. Heated on the stove, the beans wouldn't have been nearly so tasty.

During that icy condition, Steven's oral surgery appointment came due in Brandywine, sixty miles away. I tried to cancel but was told it would be months before another appointment.

My son and I headed out over the unplowed, not yet sanded, iced-over highway. Somehow we made it to Brandywine and back without leaving the road. But, on the way home Steven remarked, "Mom, I wasn't asleep." He had suffered through the entire procedure.

For the most part, our family enjoyed good health, but I still had periodic occurrences of chronic throat ulcerations, thought to be cured after the ear surgery. My ENT doctor at the base hospital said the tonsils had to be removed. The operation took place early one morning, and I woke sometime that night with a nurse sitting beside my bed. She didn't rest for the remainder of the night. Every five minutes, I called for the bedpan. She gave me tender, loving care, and said I had required blood transfusions. Recovery was painful, but the kids were in school, John was helpful with meals and cleanup, and Skipper was my sympathetic companion.

With that hurdle behind us, in the first half of 1963 we anticipated a drive, perhaps a long one, when John's assignment with the navy ended. We sold the Plymouth station wagon, bought in New York upon arrival from Pakistan, and purchased a 1955 black Chrysler Imperial from friends who had orders to Guantanamo Naval Base in Cuba. The eight-year-old car was smooth riding and had room for three kids and the dog to sit comfortably in the back seat. Johnny sat in front with us. The car was a beauty.

In May, John received orders to the Army Flight Test Activity at Edwards Air Force Base in California.

Someone on the navy base convinced him we could cross country in a travel trailer with fewer expenses. Travel from Maryland to California took six long days. Recent trips to Arkansas totaled $70 a day for food and lodging, plus fuel for the car. My husband argued a trailer would reduce our restaurant and motel costs. That appealed to him. He decided, and I suppose I went along, on the "cheaper way." We purchased a fourteen-foot Nomad travel trailer with kitchen and bath accommodations.

The kids' third year of school in Maryland ended in June. The packers came, and the moving van pulled away. We drove to the trailer dealership and loaded clothing, linens and food for the trip. John hitched our new mobile home to the eight-year-old Imperial and off we headed for the Mohave Desert, with a short stopover in Arkansas.

ADVENTURES IN THE MIDDLE OF NOWHERE

After almost three years in Maryland, where John served on a naval base, we headed west to an air force base and yet another desert. Anytime an arid-land assignment came along for an army guy, John Foster seemed the one chosen to fill it. We had lived in West Texas, in bone-dry Pakistan, and now the windblown Mohave Desert lay ahead of us. On the edge of a dry lakebed, Edwards AFB was eighty miles northeast and over the mountains from Los Angeles, and some 3,000 miles from Lexington Park, Maryland.

As we moved out with the travel trailer, I thought how convenient to have a bathroom tagging along behind us. David's bladder held for about ten miles before he began jiggling up and down behind the front seat. He refused to relieve himself on the roadside behind the open door, and his dad, who drove as though going to a fire, didn't want to stop often.

Our traveling bathroom wasn't anything to brag about. The shower was so small it required the agility of an orangutan to reach body parts. Johnny and Steven slept in the loft overhang. The dining table folded into a sleeper for Lindsey and David, and the foldout couch made into a bed for John and me. The kitchen area was outfitted with a stove, sink and fridge.

The second night out, we stopped in Arkansas, and although the trailer wasn't air conditioned, John told his dad, "It might be just the ticket. It'll save money." After short visits with our families, and learning my dad was to undergo surgery for cancer, we set out again.

I don't know where we stopped that first evening, Oklahoma City perhaps. At any rate, I broke out a large can of chicken and heated it. Along with potatoes and a salad, I thought we had a good on-the-road meal. Wow! Was I in for complaints. "I can't eat this stuff. It's awful," Johnny grumbled, and the other three kids chimed in. John and I tried, but we couldn't put it down, either. Tuna and peanut butter turned out to be winners.

Calls to Mother brought relief. Dad survived the surgery, and was recovering.

Two days later, we entered Arizona and stopped to explore the Petrified Forest, Painted Desert and Meteorite Crater. The next morning, a breakfast of scrambled eggs, bacon and pan-fried toast eaten beneath the pine-scented forest of a state park near Flagstaff more than made up for the chicken.

After our meal, we headed north to the Grand Canyon. I was surprised, for on previous moves, John had shown an unwillingness to do side trips. Perhaps there wasn't anything to see along other traveled routes, or he felt a time-related urgency about new assignments.

Over three nights of travel, my husband managed to find overnight trailer parks with electrical hook-ups and sewage dumping tanks. The last day on the road, we hit Needles, California, a nowhere-hell hole and the gateway to the Mohave Desert. Hissing vapors, the old Imperial pulled its load across the desert to Edwards without flagging in its duty. Just maybe we had this trailer travel down pat.

On the base, we were directed to a trailer parking area while awaiting the furniture van. It was a barren, sandy, desolate place. Meantime, we made a courtesy call on the Army Test Activity commander, Colonel Richard (Dick) Kennedy and his wife, Lee. Their red-haired daughter, Karen, was Lindsey's age. Next day, Lee came with cookies. Our temporary quarters weren't the most welcoming, but she graciously suffered mid-June heat in the tiny trailer space.

It wasn't a great place to keep restless kids and a hyper dachshund corralled after being cooped up in the car. Soon our furniture arrived, and we settled into our four-bedroom quarters at 6915 Balchen Drive. Johnny and Lindsey had their own bedrooms; Steven and David shared one.

A six-foot high, cinder block wall surrounded the back of every house. At one corner, a lone tree stood, and John built the kids a tree house atop the wall. The compound wall kept Skipper law-abiding. Well, most of the time.

The children had the freedom of summer ahead of them. Our military brats made friends quickly, and soon rode their bikes with other neighborhood youngsters to the Officers' pool.

We grew accustomed to sonic booms and rocket blasts rattling dishes and shaking wall hangings. The all-too-familiar desert winds and dust weren't likely to become aspects of nature we would come to appreciate.

Despite noise out of the blue and wind, we looked forward to frequent trailer adventures. Across the San Gabriel Mountains, Los Angeles sprawled for miles, inviting us to visit its many attractions. The High Sierra Mountains, San Diego, San Francisco, all lay within easy reach. Our trailer was the key to escaping another damned desert, unlike Pakistan, where the kids and I traveled no farther than fifteen miles to the beach house until we went to India.

Shortly after we arrived at Edwards, John bought a 1950 Chevrolet to get to and from the Army Test Center flight line. The used car was his treasure. He often bragged, "It's a good car. Been in the desert since new and doesn't have a rust spot anywhere."

Heat and wind persisted into September when schools opened. Desert High was across the street and three compound walls away. Our thirteen-year-old Johnny, a seventh grader, and other Balchen Street students, chose walking on compound walls over walking the streets to the high school. Lindsey, a fifth grader, Steven fourth, and David third, rode their bikes to Forbes Elementary not far from our house, and in the same school complex as Desert High.

One day, they came from school, tossed their books aside and called, "Mom, a snake is lying on the front landing." Running into the garage, I snatched up a rake and hacked the eight-inch demon to death. Eve's revenge.

With school in session, I volunteered at the base hospital, and soon was active in both the Army and Air Force Wives' Clubs. Shopping at the commissary always took a weekday morning. Besides the hospital and commissary, Edwards offered an NCO Club, a gas station, a fast food eatery, drive-in movie, dry cleaning-laundry house, and a large store stocked with thought-to-be essential items. Instead of the end of the line, as in Maryland, we were in the middle of nowhere.

For the first time in years, I hired a housekeeper. Mia was an excellent cleaning lady. On November 2, 1963, she and I went about our tasks when Johnny rushed from school at lunchtime. "President Kennedy was shot," he blurted. For the next week, I watched televised events leading to the assassinated president being laid to rest in Arlington National Cemetery. It was one of the saddest times in my life.

Johnny had a lot of friends, but his best friend, Rob Storm, lived across the street from us. Rob's sister, Peggy, and our son had a sort of "first attraction" thing going.

Lindsey's best friend, Tamara, lived across Balchen. Our daughter fed Tamara's dog when the family went away for a weekend. It bit Lindsey and had to be quarantined. Friendship between the girls cooled. Soon Tamara's father received orders, and the family moved.

The Ambos, a Japanese couple, acquired the vacant quarters. Their son, Dickey, became Steven and David's friend. An inventive-sort, Dickey made an amplifier out of John's stereo using two bobby pins with the rubber tips removed. Apparently, Dickey lacked voice talent, as did our David. The two boys auditioned for Steve's instrumental band. Both were rejected by the band members.

Steve played his drum ensemble and three other boys had guitars. If the group was anything, it was loud. They practiced in our garage with amplifiers full bore. On a Sunday afternoon, John and I took

Skipper for a walk. A couple of blocks from our house, one of the neighbors ran out to meet us on the sidewalk. "If you don't end that noise, I'm going to call the MPs (military police)." The band moved to some other parent's garage.

While Steven expressed himself musically, Lindsey lacked the desire. We purchased a new Baldwin spinet piano for her. Her California music teacher tried to drum music theory into her head. Our daughter never said so, but I imagined her urge to tell me that she never wanted to be a musician and didn't understand why I thought she should take lessons.

Johnny decided the cornet was his instrument.

Christmas came, and we give ourselves a family gift, a color TV set. We went to Arkansas with small gifts to open under grandparents' Yule trees. Back in California, John closed-in the outdoor patio. With re-covered cushions on the wrought iron pieces, purchased in Texas, and the new TV, we furnished our den.

Mild weather allowed John and Johnny to spend weekends tearing the Chevy's engine apart and putting it back together. At fourteen our son dreamed of the time when he could drive a car. He liked mechanical work and enjoyed pastimes that engaged his hands.

John and I took him to the Riverside Race Track one Saturday. Engine and crowd clatter, plus gas fumes were enough for me, but John took him on other occasions. Johnny liked California. He enjoyed desert flowers and the open starlit sky.

One day after school, he and Rob rode their bikes to the "essentials" store. They came home with candy bars. I knew my son was penniless, and he admitted to snitching when the clerk wasn't looking. "Well, young man, you're taking the candy back, admitting what you did, and apologizing." Off we went. I was a mean mother, but proud of my son for 'fessing up to the storekeeper.

His misbehavior reminded me of being with a classmate who filched a bag of Jelly Beans while the butcher cut her mother's meat order. When we stepped out on the sidewalk, she showed me the bag of candy. I helped eat the Jelly Beans even though scared out of my wits that we would be caught. I carried that load of guilt for a few years.

Another year of school meant shopping for clothing. The kids and I headed for Lancaster, the nearest town, intending to shop at Sears. We had just left the base when the hood on the Imperial popped up in front of the windshield, blocking my view. I pulled off the road, and Johnny helped me try to force it down. We couldn't budge it. Turning around, I drove home with my head hanging out the window.

Trips to buy clothing were necessary, but adventure trips were few and far between. "We can go on fun trips," John had said when we bought the trailer. Early on, we managed to get away a few times, but during four and a half years at Edwards, John was tied to test programs, some in the mountains for high altitude testing. On rare, free weekends, we headed out in the Imperial with the Nomad trailing behind. Destinations: Death Valley, the mountains or a California city.

We heard about Apple Valley, an hour's drive south of the air force base. Lindsey and David always felt a bit cheated as their birthdays were just before and after Christmas.

On David's special day, we went to Apple Valley, the land of Roy Rogers, the movie cowboy. Our son wasn't impressed with a life-sized replica of Roy's horse, Trigger, or the frontier wagons spread about.

The day was quite cool, and I made hot soup for the thermos and sandwiches for a picnic. Just as we were ready to eat, a sudden desert deluge rained down on us. We ran to the car. Crowded three to a seat, we jiggled cups of soup and tried to eat sandwiches. John grumbled, "I don't like eating in the car." None of us did that day.

If there had been interesting things on-going in Apple Valley, we might have enjoyed the moments, and let them pass from memory. Because this was one of the least pleasant excursions, it was cemented in our minds. Any reminder of that day, at family gatherings, brought laughter.

On another excursion, the Imperial pulled the trailer onto an entrance ramp to a Los Angeles Freeway and stalled. It suffered vapor lock. We sat there on the precarious edge of a busy roadway, waiting for the old girl's engine to cool down, and expecting any minute to be rear-ended by an up-ramp vehicle, or squashed by on-coming traffic.

One of our outings took us to a small brick building in the mountains. With no other buildings around for miles, it appeared deserted, but a railroad ran behind it. Curious, John pulled in front. After concluding it must be a station where skiers left the train for the slopes, John started backing our rig to turn around. Suddenly, we noticed nothing but sky behind us. Our butts were so close to hanging over the sheer edge of the mesa, it brought our hearts up in our throats.

There were other heart-stopping occasions. The faithful old car huffed and puffed up yet another mountain, and around a sharp curve before she gave up. Three of the kids and I sat in the car while John stood at one end of the curve, and Johnny at the other, directing traffic around us. At last "Smokey the Bear" came along in a National Park truck and pulled car, trailer and us across the mountain to safety.

Then, the time came when we drove up Green Mountain to retrieve Lindsey from a Girl Scout camp. It was a day trip, no trailer in tow. Returning down the mountain, we stopped at several overlooks to take in views. At one sight, Skipper found a varmint hole and began digging. Bred to hunt badgers, he made a mound of dirt, which led us to him. He was so deep in the hole, only his tail was visible. He wasn't happy about being extracted before reaching his prey.

We all piled back in the car, and our vehicle waited for a steep descent before sending yet another distress signal. Suddenly, John in his unflappable way, said, "I think our brakes are gone." We panicked while he put the Imperial in low gear and let her rip. At the bottom, the car rolled to a stop, and we caught our breaths.

Every one of our adventures proved to be a struggle for the Imperial, but we paid little heed to her warnings and made another trip to Arkansas with the grand old gal towing the trailer. We didn't make it back to Edwards before Skipper, angry at being left in the car while we had a restaurant meal, took several large chunks of leather and foam stuffing out of the back seat.

If our old Imperial could have spoken, what tales she would have told. She surely would have beeped her horn to let us know Johnny and his friend were on a joy ride in her.

Our son neared the age for a driver's license. During his Drivers' Ed course at Desert High, it fell my duty to ride with him, as he practiced driving skills in an empty parking lot.

I wasn't the best person for this parental challenge, and he was yelled at more than once.

We attended a crowded school event in the gym the evening he decided to solo. Over the speaker system came, "Will Major Foster meet the MPs at the front of the gym?"

They took John to their vehicle, where Johnny and Rob were held.

John's calm acceptance of our fifteen-year-old being nabbed while driving without a license amazed me. I wasn't so kind. Clearly, there was a lack of understanding on my part about the adventurous nature of male teenagers. I had heard, "There is one in every family." Loveable Johnny was our daring teen, and my parental challenge.

After he earned his license, the police picked up Johnny again. This time he wasn't the driver, but was with a group of his school buddies. It happened to be on an evening when we had the Baptist chaplain, his wife and son as dinner guests. They lived up the street from us, and Bill, the son, was Steven's friend.

The phone rang during dinner. The MPs were on the other end of the line. They had stopped the boys, found a six-pack of beer in the car, and hauled them into the station. John left our curious guests to see about bailing our child out of jail. He and Johnny didn't return before our visitors departed. With concern and curiosity, the chaplain asked if there was anything they could do. "Do you want us to stay with you?" Having learned nothing about the situation despite their inquisitive efforts, they finally went home.

When John returned with Johnny, he said the MPs gave the boys a lecture and released them into parental custody. Our son was giving us a lot of lessons about raising our first teenager.

While we tried to control him, it was a bit touchier with a friend in our Army Test Activity group who encroached on my time. She was sort of a "know-it-all," who enjoyed spreading a full report every morning. The kitchen phone's long extension cord let me reach the front entrance and ring the doorbell. "Sorry, dear, someone's at the door." A quick hang up was used often enough without blowing my excuse, and we remained friends. Military relationships were that way, steadfast, sadly, even when a deceased's name appeared in *Cockpit*, a quarterly publication.

With some control over a friend whom I didn't wish to hurt, it clearly was time to consider selling our beautiful, black, chrome-fitted, 1955 Imperial. Many a time it had signaled it was about to have a nervous breakdown. "The dear old thing should be let go gracefully." We went to Los Angeles and traded her for a new International Travel-All.

In my mind, the only favorable thing going for the T-A was its power to pull the trailer. It rode like a truck, roared like a truck; it was a truck.

As it turned out, we had fewer opportunities to travel. Test programs took John on TDYs or tied him to the base. No kind of prize would have enticed me to drive with the trailer in tow and our kids in the car. Not even without the kids.

With a third seat facing the rear window, the T-A could haul eight passengers. A plus when Mother and Dad came for a visit. On a Sunday morning, we rushed from church to the small, isolated, yellow train station some five miles across the dry lakebed. A sign on one end of the building read, "Edwards." It was imperative that we arrive ahead of my parents' train. "Hurry John, if we aren't there when the train stops, Dad will take one look and say, 'Era, there isn't anything around here but that building. We're not getting off this train.'"

We arrived just ahead of their conveyance. Dad confirmed, "I wouldn't have dismounted that iron horse if I hadn't seen ya'll."

They kept us in stitches with stories about the rail ride from Arkansas.

Dad especially enjoyed their seating assignments. The conductor put them in the same car, but Dad was up front next to a pretty lady. Mother sat alone toward the back. She tolerated the situation for a while then marched up to the woman and claimed her husband. The lady graciously exchanged seats.

Mom took more pleasure in telling about Dad shedding his shoes before taking a nap. When he woke, his shoes were missing. Looking up and down the aisle, he found another man wearing them. Dad's shoes had "walked" toward the front of the car, and a gent, who also removed his shoes, put on the handiest pair.

On their first visit to California, Disneyland proved a bit much for my parents, but visits with Mother's Los Angeles cousins, not seen since childhood, pleased her. She had a ride down Hollywood and Vine Streets, and sat in the Hollywood Bowl.

Sometime after they returned to Arkansas, we made our annual trip to visit them and John's parents. We headed south to Palm Springs and on eastward, picking up an interstate and landing in Yuma, Arizona, at the end of the first day. John pulled the T-A and trailer into an RV park. The temperature registered three digits. My husband connected the electricity, water and sewage, then he and the kids grabbed their swim gear and went to the pool. Skipper ran right behind them, and without hesitation, he jumped into the pool, too.

One of the kids brought the wet dog back to the trailer, where together, he and I made dinner in the Styxian-like inferno. "Yep, one of those 'cheap' journeys John found so appealing," I mumbled, and wiped sweat. That night, after everyone cooled with a shower and hit the beds, I lay awake wondering why we chose a southern route in summertime.

In the morning, Steve said, "I sat up all night in the open loft window, trying to breathe." No one had slept well.

We left Yuma, remembering it as another hellhole in our adventures, swearing never to go there again. But Arizona peaks, desert plants, and Indian ruins left a pleasant indent in our memory banks.

In El Paso, we had a Tex-Mex dinner with the Bensons, whom we'd not seen since Pakistan. Leaving there, we made it to Houston for a short visit with my cousins, the Simpsons, then on to Lewisville.

On the way back to California, somewhere in the mountains along I-40, the trailer began a downhill sashay that scared the bee-gees out of us. John brought it under control, but I wasn't having any more of that. "As soon as we get home, this rig is history. Travel-All and trailer. We can stay in a lot of motels for what we've paid for these road hogs."

Despite my declaration, we didn't get rid of the travel rig right away. We made a trip in the mountains to a place where John and the kids fished for trout. On the way home, we came upon a small village beside the Kern River. My husband pulled off, and we sat in the T-A watching inner tube-floaters wade into the river and start their ride downstream.

It was a hot day and after a few minutes, John drove on. We had gone a short distance when Lindsey asked, "Where are Steve and David?" I told her to check the seat facing the rear window. "Mom, they aren't back there." Steven was almost nine, and David would be eight in December. My heart felt like it would implode.

We had gone about ten miles from the river stop, when John turned around and retraced the seemingly longest distance ever. Across the sun-heated street from the stopover place, we spotted our little guys seated on chain-linked, wooden posts, marking the front boundary of a motel. They dangled seared bare feet. Using good judgment, they didn't appear upset, and had waited for us to return.

Another winter came, and we collected up the sleds, our kids, one of Johnny's friends, and Skipper, and headed for the snow-covered mountains above Tehachapi. If we had owned one more sled, I would have bellied-down on it and joined in the seasonal fun. Instead, Skipper and I sat on the sideline and watched the others speed past us while John recorded the pleasurable afternoon on his camera.

Not long after, we parked the Travel-All and trailer in our driveway, and put a "For Sale" sign on them. Soon, there was a buyer for both. We went to Los Angeles and selected a white 1965 Chrysler Imperial, large enough to seat six and the dog. Like the faithful old black car, it was a beauty, and on the next trip across the mountains to Arkansas, we had a fun encounter with a Volkswagen. The young driver passed us going downhill, and we sped past him on I-40's inclines. The game went on for miles. He spread a priceless grin each time he rolled past our big car and when the kids giggled and waved as we finally left him behind.

On this trip, we stopped at a service station and were almost back on the interstate ramp when looking back, I saw Lindsey walking from the restroom with a bewildered look on her face. Oops, we didn't count heads, or maybe we counted Skipper. Service station attendants often said they mistook our dog for a person as he sat upright with a paw on the armrest.

Later, driving on into the western mountains, John noticed a low reading on the gas gage. He drove on and on, until it showed way past empty. Luck was with us. We topped a hill and coasted down into a service station. Always aware of the lack of stations across the western half of the country, we pondered how we were caught in such a situation.

Before we made it home, the car had some kind of breakdown. It was pouring rain. A kind person stopped, learned of our problem and went on ahead to a service station. A tow truck arrived, and the driver hoisted the rear of our car upward, leaving us to ride on a slant and facing backward to a garage in a nearby town. People in passing cars stared at us. At family gatherings, retelling this incident evoked an image that always caused hysterical laughter.

Back at Edwards, my husband carried out test projects that could and often did last for a month or more away from home. When our men were home, someone usually had a party for the group. On one of those occasions, we left the three younger kids in Johnny's care. Before we sat down to our hostess' dinner, there was a call. "David blew in Skipper's ear, and he bit him on the mouth," Johnny reported.

We rushed home, and John took David to the hospital. We knew the hospital would report the bite, and Skipper would be quarantined. Our whole family went into upset-mode. "John you must do something.

Skipper's never been away for so long without seeing us. He'll bark himself to death."

We implored my husband and their dad to take action. Next morning John was on the phone to the chief of medical affairs.

"There isn't any way I can avoid reporting your dog to the MPs," he said.

John went up the chain of command, calling one high-ranking person after the other, finally ending with the base commander. He agreed to let Skipper stay in our compound for fourteen days.

Our dachshund escaped arrest for that mishap, but there was the time he slipped out of the compound after someone left the gate open. I stood on the corner calling, when up the sidewalk I saw him trotting along at the tail end of a pack of dogs. Skipper was half a block away, when suddenly the MPs appeared out of nowhere. "Hurry, Skipper. Run!" I called at the top of my voice.

His short little legs pumped as hard as he could go, but not fast enough. He was the only dog in the pack nabbed and taken to the pound.

On Sunday after church, we drove to a hilltop overlooking the pound about two blocks below. Skipper was having a jumping-barking hissy, just as we thought he would. I went for him on Monday morning. He bounced from front to back seat, yelping all the way home. I was ready to do away with our best friend.

If it wasn't our dog, it was our lovable eldest kid. At fourteen, he had grown a mustache. Mean mom made him shave before going to church. Then the Beatles came from England to America's musical stage and made an instant impression on our Johnny. At sixteen, he grew Beatle-style hair. School opened and his hair violated the dress code. He was expelled.

His dad was away on TDY, so it fell my duty to talk the school official into letting him off the hook. "He will get a haircut," I promised. Johnny reluctantly took a haircut and returned to school. However, he didn't understand why hair grown to the tops of his ears was undesirable. It didn't look unkempt, and I agreed without him knowing.

Soon, we said goodbye to Colonel and Mrs. Kennedy, who left for another assignment. They were replaced by the next Army Test Activity commander, Colonel Zornig and his wife, Phyllis.

Around this time, I took a complaint to one of the doctors whom I assisted at the hospital. He sent me to March AFB for tests. Ann Masters rode with me to the base near San Bernardino. One phase of the examination left an unforgettable imprint—the Lower GI Series. Dressed in the white, open-back gown tied at the nape, I took the barium enema in a room almost a block away from the restroom. On a hard run down the hall, my gown tails flapping, I passed waiting patients lining the walls. At that moment, the least of my worries was what they might see.

To relieve my tension, Ann and I shopped in Los Angeles before heading home.

Back at Edwards, my doctor said, "You need gall bladder surgery." My small complaint had been a sore spot in the abdominal area. I never had symptoms related to the gall bladder, and suspected my doctor of wanting to hone his surgical skills. Nevertheless, the surgery took place, and a year later another surgery for hernia repair. Was this another case of practicing the profession? For someone who appeared in good health, I also had a bout with pneumonia following a visit to Arkansas.

While seeing after our children was my primary concern, words still presented a certain fascination for me. A desire to write was strong, and I enrolled in the Famous Writers fiction-writing course. Soon, it was obvious that I didn't write all that well, but story ideas came readily. At the end of the correspondence course, I wasn't sure my writing was much improved, but I learned a great deal about writing techniques.

In 1965 as I tried to satisfy a creative desire, John accomplished his own noteworthy feat. He broke the helicopter speed record previously held by the Russians. It got attention. There were news articles, recognition at a formal awards ceremony in Los Angeles, and an appearance on *To Tell The Truth*, the television show hosted by

Gary Moore. None of the panelists, Bill Cullen, Kitty Carlisle, Henry Morgan, and Florence Henderson—filling in for Peggy Cass— guessed that John's line was that of a test pilot. He returned home with a prize of one hundred dollars.

Breaking the speed record led John back to Arkansas where he was honored as a "native son" of our hometown at a Lewisville Chamber of Commerce annual dinner.

Little did we realize after all the recognition that we would awake one morning to quite a different experience. John left before daylight without waking me. From the flight line, he and an engineer, George Yamakowa, flew out in an UH1-D helicopter. They had flown the test the day before, and this was to be a repeat, because workers had improperly installed instruments, and the oscillograph tracings had not recorded.

The chopper was reloaded with machine guns and rockets, instrumentation, and bags of lead pebbles behind the cockpit seats for testing the craft's endurance under weighted conditions.

Out over the desert, John carried out test maneuvers as his engineer took notes for the program write-up. During an auto-rotation maneuver, John cut the engine at a certain altitude to test the helicopter under its load. At a certain descent point, he cranked the throttle to restart, but the engine failed to catch. The craft hit the desert floor, and skipped over land with spinning rotor blades striking the ground. My husband was thrown through the glass cockpit between the moving blades. Still strapped in his seat, he tumbled over land for about fifty feet.

When he stopped rolling, he unbuckled, looked back at the wreck and saw the engineer rising up in the cockpit, and shaking off broken glass. Although in extreme pain and blood running from his chin, John hobbled back and helped his engineer away from the chopper just before it caught fire.

The two of them sat down some distance from the crash and watched the flying machine burn. They waited, knowing that a pilot would be sent out to look for them when they didn't return to the base within a reasonable time. Meantime, a farmer who lived nearby had seen the craft go down. He drove up in his truck, and took them back to his house. From there they called the Army Test Center, and Major Jim Honaker was sent in a helicopter to take them to the base hospital.

That morning, I saw the kids off to school, dressed in my Gray Lady uniform, and drove to the hospital. I was on volunteer duty about an hour, when one of four outpatient doctors I served stood at his office door and motioned me to follow him inside. Wondering if I had made a mistake, I entered and was invited to sit.

"Your husband was in a plane crash. He's not seriously injured," he said as I began to hyperventilate. "Has a sprained ankle, bruises, and a gashed chin. You can visit him upstairs."

After a stay in the hospital, John was released to recover at home for about a month. He had a host of visitors each day.

Following his recovery, he was promoted to lieutenant colonel. For some time we knew he was on the promotion list, but didn't know when it would happen. On a morning when Army Test Activity wives were to host the Air Force Wives Club coffee, I was in charge of our set-up committee at the Officers' Club. We took silver tea and coffee services to the dressed tables when I was called to the phone. Colonel Leonard Dennis at the Test Center said, "You should drive over for the promotion ceremony and assist me in pinning on John's silver oak leaves."

I left the girls setting up the coffee and attended the ceremony. Returning to the club just as the social meeting ended, we cleaned up and restored coffee services to their proper places. By that time, it was three o'clock. I left on a run to the base store. Back in the car with needed items for serving our guests at the promotion party that evening, I raced toward home. Suddenly red lights flashed behind the car. "You were speeding," the MP said. After a warning, he let me go.

The kids arrived from school as I called wives who did not attend the coffee to invite them to the party. Next was a call to the bartender, whom I had engaged earlier and warned of short notice. With the kids fed, I threw together finger food and told the bartender where to set up. All was ready when John came home and guests began to arrive. What a day!

Soon after John's promotion, the Zornigs were replaced by Colonel John Elliott and his wife, whom I immediately admired. Colonel Zornig was an all right-kind of guy, but Mrs. Zornig, a former school teacher, tended to treat wives as though we were her students.

We lived on Edwards Air Force Base from June 1963 until November 1967—the longest military tour to that date—when John received orders.

He sold his prized 1950 green Chevy to Colonel Elliott. To his regret, for I was the one who said, "We will not need that car in Lewisville." Hindsight proved me wrong, for Johnny would need a car.

There was the usual farewell party where John was presented a framed piece of molten metal from the remains of the crashed helicopter. The metal resembled a piece of sculpture. Another gift was a framed caricature of my husband, feet propped upon his desk, arms clasped behind his head. The artist, Porque Orgus, was an illustrator for the Army Test Activity. All of John's fellow Test Center people autographed both items.

The ladies presented me with a silver tray, etched with the Army Wives Club name and dates. Most of us had been together for four-and-a half years, and it was an emotional parting.

Our departure was also a dreaded one. John was going to Vietnam, and he wanted us to live in Lewisville while he was away. I was happy to leave California. The packers came, and the movers loaded the van. An air force vehicle picked up the kids and drove them to the Los Angeles airport. They flew to Texarkana where my mother awaited their arrival.

DAD GOES TO VIETNAM

The moving van pulled away, and John and I drove off Edwards Air Force Base. After four-and-a-half years of calling it home, we began the three-day drive to Arkansas.

When we arrived, Mother had the kids in school, the same school John and I had graduated from in the Forties. Johnny was a junior and Lindsey a freshman in Lewisville High. Steve and David were junior high students.

Before she picked up the kids at the airport, my mom had spread the word that her grandchildren were coming to live in our small town. Full of excitement, they told us how they were received. "The first day in school," Lindsey said in disbelief, "all these kids rushed up and greeted us by our first names. Wow! We felt popular right from the beginning. Kids ride past the house, honking their horns and waving."

For all their young lives, our four had left friends and faced making new ones. Left teachers and adapted to new ones. Now they were in for a small town experience in which everyone had known everyone else for lifetimes, or for most of their lives.

I was as happy as the kids to be in my town, and what would we have done without my mom? I doubt that I expressed appreciation clearly enough for her to get it. Not only did she see to the children but she found a house and arranged with the seller for us to purchase it. The neat three-bedroom, two-bath brick on the corner of Sixth and Steel Streets, sat across

Sixth from the city water tower. In a few days, the van pulled in front, and we crowded six people and our dachshund into our new home.

Once we were settled, John and I made plans to enlarge the house to fit our needs. He hired his cousin, Bob Barmes, to turn the one-car garage into a bedroom for Steven and David.

With the conversion completed, the builder began a carport on the back of the house, extending the roof over the existing patio to connect with the storage room. The shower in the bath off the master bedroom was replaced later.

A chain link fence surrounded the back yard, just the right place for Skipper to romp about, so we thought. Within days, he fooled us by digging beneath the fence to freedom. John fixed that problem by laying a cement pad under the complete length of the enclosure.

With the house in order, my husband began a five-month period of travel to Fort Benning, Georgia, before leaving for his overseas tour. Sending whole units to Vietnam was a recently developed concept, and it required a great deal of preparation. John and two other Army officers, each with responsibility for two airfield support units, prepared the troops by assigning their overseas duties and seeing to their Vietnam readiness.

He returned home every other weekend, and sometime in the five-month period before shipping out, he and our eldest son went to Shreveport to purchase a used car for Johnny. They drove into the driveway with a 1946 Ford sedan. I went ballistic.

"But that's what he wanted. An antique car," my husband explained.

"A 20-year-old automobile! I doubt I can drive the thing." John drove our family car back and forth to Georgia, and I used my parents' 1965 Ford with gearshift on the steering column and requiring clutching. Until I drove their car, it had been more than ten years since I clutched and shifted the Blue Bomber and the station wagon. Now, I had the challenge of a 1946 vehicle.

After many jerks and forward leaps, I relearned clutching and shifting.

Lindsey was in Driver's Ed class. One Sunday afternoon, we took Johnny's Ford on a country road to give her practice. Coming to a sharp curve, she didn't make the turn, and we landed in a wooded area. Rain had left the ground slick. After much rev-ing of the engine and spinning, we broke pine limbs to place behind the back tires. Soon we were back on the road, but Johnny's car was covered in mud.

We stopped at my parents' home for a short visit, after which Dad walked to the car with us. "Where did you get all the mud?" We told him what happened, and Lindsey asked that he not tell Johnny. Back home, we washed his Ford, and her brother never knew about the accident.

John came home for a month's leave before accompanying soldiers in the airfield units on a ship cruise to Vietnam. When he departed in April 1968, all the work on the house was completed with the exception of the bathroom shower.

Left to oversee the shower installation, I was also knee-deep in teenagers. It was a time when apron strings needed to be loosened while maintaining a loose knot of control. Again, we settled into living without a father and husband. The children seemed to accept this as a normal way of life. Now at independent stages, they spent much of their free time with friends. I was left with Skipper. We took walks, and he rode with me to the post office to mail letters to John.

I made monthly runs to the Barksdale Air Force Base Commissary and Base Exchange. The round-trip to Shreveport covered one hundred-twenty miles and a day's worth of time.

Lewisville wasn't a busy place. Only a few of the people I had grown up with still lived there. Other than attending services at the First Baptist Church—the church of my childhood and youth—there was little social activity. Friends invited me to attend a liquid embroidery class. While pleased to be included, my hands didn't do artsy works, such as painting beautiful designs on cloth with liquid colors.

While I couldn't paint, I still wanted the kids to be musical. All three boys had instruments. Johnny had a cornet, but I can't remember him playing with the band, more than likely because football practice interfered. Steve played drums in a small band for dances at the Teen Club. Both he and David, on the baritone, were in the school band. Lindsey's piano teacher was Mrs. Mataleah Searcy. She was the Glee Club pianist when I was in high school.

I was grateful for visits by her, Miss Marjorie Walker, and Mrs. Aline Landes, all of whom had taught John and me. Then, there was John's Uncle Edwin, a handyman about town. He dropped by often to ask if repairs were needed. I knew this kind man stopped in just to see if we fared well.

The kids led active lives. Johnny was on the football team and drove Robin, a new girlfriend, around town in his antique car. Lindsey went on dates with her first boyfriend, Jerry, and her tight-knit clique of girlfriends were always up to something. Steve fancied a girl who lived on a farm west of town. He didn't drive, so I suppose they hung out at school. David and his good friend, Larry, played junior varsity basketball.

With all their activities, it was Johnny who demonstrated the most concern for his father. He was always one to share his opinion, albeit in a respectful manner. One day in class, he voiced his objection to the Vietnam War. He hadn't made many points with the teacher who listened, then said, "You're just a Communist."

My son was apparently hurt but undaunted. "Mr. ____, I have to remind you that my dad is in Vietnam fighting against Communism."

I formed my own opinion about that man, a pompous jackass, who called himself a teacher. My kids, all of whom had him in some capacity or another, told stories of his feet propped upon the desk as he asked students to read the next chapter in the book.

It came Junior Prom time, and Johnny took Robin in the Imperial. A classmate of Johnny's invited Lindsey, and I talked her into accepting because the kid didn't have a date. My daughter marked an indelible X in her mind next to mom's name so as not to forget that one.

When school recessed for summer, Johnny set out to every place in town that might need seasonal help. At each business, he was told, "We've already hired Robert." Or James, or whomever. Jobs went to kids who held them the summer before. Finally, my son was hired on a farm, baling hay in the southern Arkansas heat.

He had never done manual labor, but stuck with it until the two of us had an argument over the air-conditioner. The A-C went on the blink, and I turned it off, warning the kids not to turn it on before the repairman came. "It will be several days before I can get to it," he said, "but it sounds like the unit is freezing up." Water saturated the carpet. I put down towels and turned on an oscillating fan.

The next day, I drove to Barksdale, and when I returned tired from grocery shopping, the air-conditioner was running. Johnny took a scolding up one side and down the other.

The following morning, I went for an appointment. Back home, the three kids met me. "Johnny's gone. He's driving to California in his car."

In a 20-year-old vehicle! Only another mother would know such fear. My son left with $70 in his pocket. I had no way to reach him other than to call the police to locate and return him. That would further humiliate my seventeen-year-old. Always of tender heart, he left a sweet note for me, trying to explain himself.

On his third night out, I knew he would be near Flagstaff, Arizona, if all went well. Around three o'clock in the morning, I woke. Pacing the living room, I prayed. At some point, I suddenly felt relief flow into my mind, and knew my son was all right.

Not long after Johnny left, I answered the door one night. It was John's cousin, Tommy. "I just caught a bunch of kids in the swimming pool. It's closed, and they jumped over the fence. Your daughter was with them."

I had never met Tommy, but I was grateful that he had told me about Lindsey's misdeed. She was grounded for a week, the only one of her confederates in misbehavior to be punished, and another X was marked next my name.

I had no one to turn to, not my parents nor John's. They were a generation removed from the problems Johnny confronted. He left behind many friends and Dee, his first girlfriend in California. Apparently, severing those friendships was heart wrenching for him.

Finally, I turned to his English teacher, a single mother trying to raise a teenaged daughter. Johnny was quite fond of Mrs. Christie, but when I shared my son's flight to California, she offered sympathy and fear for my child, something I didn't need. I don't know what I expected from friends and family, perhaps reassurance he would return.

At last I received a call from his former girlfriend. He had made it to Edwards AFB in that old car.

Johnny had been away six weeks, and school would open in two weeks, when he called. "I want to come home, Mom. I have a friend with me. He's been thrown out of his house. May I bring him?"

He could have asked to bring Satan, and the response would have been the same. "Of course, come home, Johnny." Four days later, they arrived looking every bit the "hippies" they were trying to emulate with long hair, dirty clothes and bare feet.

Before school opened, I planned to take the other three kids and several of their friends— Lindsey's boyfriend and Steve's classmate, Brian Dennington—to the 1968 Hemisphere Fair in San Antonio. Johnny and his friend didn't want to go. We left them at home and spent three or four days in the Texas city, sharing time at the fair with the Bensons, friends from Pakistan. We saw the Alamo, and on the way home drove through Austin for a tour of the state capitol.

I had not driven far out of Austin when my left arm began to ache. Placing it on the armrest, I drove on for a while before asking Lindsey's boyfriend to get us home.

The painful ache continued several days, having switched to the right arm. Other symptoms such as body ache, headache and fatigue set in. After a number of visits to our family doctor, he said, "I don't know what your problem is, and I don't have the equipment to test you. Can you be at the hospital in the morning?" He made an appointment with a neurologist in Shreveport and reserved my room at Schumpert Hospital.

By that time, I was almost totally incapacitated and had called John's aunt to come help out. The next morning, she, my dad and I loaded into the car with Johnny behind the wheel. I had made a shopping list for Aunt Viola and my son to fill at the commissary. We stopped there first.

The three of us went inside to explain my situation to the commissary manager, and to show my military identification card. My condition was quite evident, and the manager readily agreed for Aunt Viola and Johnny to return after dropping me at the hospital.

Johnny pulled into the emergency entrance, and someone met me with a wheelchair. Dad and Aunt Viola accompanied me inside, while my son parked the car. I was rolled away, leaving Dad to admit me.

I don't remember much after that. While I was under heavy sedation, the doctors carried out a number of tests without reaching a diagnosis.

I don't know how long I had been in the hospital when one night I woke to see a nurse at my bedside. Mother called. I tried to respond, but my sentences were nonsensical. The nurse took the phone and explained I had just awakened from an arteriogram in which dye was directed through an artery into my brain. Hanging up, she helped me through a night of vomiting.

The last test, a spinal tap, determined I had viral encephalitis, the result of a mosquito bite. The diagnosis brought relief, for I feared a brain tumor. The doctor must have suspected that as well, else why the arteriogram?

I begged to be released, telling the doctor that John was in Vietnam and my teenagers needed me. He warned I wasn't yet fit, but he would allow it only if I had help. Assured that I did, he gave permission. Johnny came for me. By this time his California friend had left Lewisville.

At home, Aunt Viola said, "John's mother is quite ill, and she needs my help."

The four kids had little understanding of my limitations. Without help, I soon regressed to the point of fearing a return to the hospital. I called my aunt in Little Rock.

Aunt Nelle was childless, but wise and had a disposition I could trust. She took charge of the situation. Calling her great niece and nephews into a room, she explained my problem in a convincing manner and made them understand they must help. My problem was solved.

Mother brought soup, and Dad often stopped to visit on his runs downtown. We had long talks, and I came to really know my father. Our parents raised my brother and me in the manner of their time, and I followed right down that authoritative path. Johnny's leaving for California jarred me into reviewing my methods.

For the next three months, I could only stay up for short periods. During this time a friend, Corrine Ford McGee, visited. Some eight years older than I, she was a widow with her share of problems in raising three youngsters, one of whom was Johnny's age. Sometime during our conversation, she said, "No matter what they do, all you can do is love your children." It was a simple statement. Of course, I loved my children, but her words struck a chord.

I needed someone to let me know that I wasn't the only person going through a difficult patch. Her visit helped me toward recovery. I felt lucky to have an aunt and a friend at just the right time of need.

It was a while before Johnny felt he could tell me about his stay in California. He and his friend had worked at a potato processing location, probably some place near Bakersfield and not far from Edwards. I'm sure lack of money kept them from traveling any distance. My son told about sacking potatoes for shipment, and spending nights trying to sleep on the bagged tubers. I couldn't bring myself to ask how he fed himself those many days. Looking back, dare I say as difficult as that period was, it appears to have been a good lesson for both of us.

With opening of school, our lives fell into a normal routine.

In October, John's week of Rest and Recreation (R&R) in Hawaii was scheduled. I called another of John's aunts to stay with the kids, and while not completely recovered, I flew out of Dallas on the way to meet him.

Frankie Rhodes, who had children in Dallas, accompanied me on the drive to Texas. We arrived at the Grays' home in Irving, and I stayed overnight with them. The next day, Ruth and her friend's husband took me to the airport.

I landed in Honolulu a day ahead of John, and was transported to the designated R&R, beach hotel. The next morning, a military person called to say John had landed and would arrive at the hotel momentarily. From my room, I heard the elevator and ran out to greet my husband. Both hands held his bags, and before he could drop them, I thrust myself at him. "Wait!" he said, letting the bags fall to the floor. He may not have meant it to sting, but it did. Waiting was the game that dominated my life.

Fatigue limited what I could do. We toured the island of Oahu by bus, saw Pearl Harbor, walked on beaches, enjoyed a luau, envied hula dancers and macho men climbing great heights up palm trees to collect coconuts. Unable to motor far, I sat on sidewalk benches, periodically.

We had an unforgettable experience with a kind Japanese woman. After a morning in a sprawling, new mall, purchasing gifts to take back home, we walked to the street corner and waited for a bus. A Mercedes pulled to the curb. The lady rolled down the window and called, "Where are you going?" We told her, and she invited, "Come, I will take you right there." She went out of her way to drop us at our destination. I'm sure my husband's uniform invited her kind deed.

When our week ended at the Honolulu airport, I was given the customary lei, and in late evening, John saw me off. Seated behind me, two men kept their light on and talked all night. Upon leaving the plane at the Los Angeles airport satellite drop, I fell asleep while waiting for the shuttle to take me to the terminal. Awaking in time, I made my connection to Dallas.

Football was well into the season, when I arrived home. A friend told me that Johnny made a deciding touchdown while I was away. He hadn't mentioned his accomplishment. I was proud of him and felt badly that I had missed it.

One Devils' game took place at a school near Hot Springs. Lindsey and I rode up together, and Steven and David went on the band bus. We watched Johnny's team compete up to half time, when the Lewisville High School Band marched onto the field to perform. The drums beat, the horns tooted and feet marched. Suddenly, we spectators realized the formation had gone awry. Band members were all over the field, still beating and tooting. Then, just as the marching feet had veered out of formation, they fell back into an orderly march off the field. It was unbelievable.

The homecoming game was ahead. Lindsey was one of four homecoming maids, one of whom would be crowned the school queen. She didn't get to wear the crown as I had in 1946, but she rode in a parade through town, a privilege I didn't have.

In my day, there wasn't a football team. I was crowned in the school auditorium during intermission of the junior class play.

My daughter wore a beautiful gown, but when I was chosen, the war had just ended, and I was lucky to find a formal dress. My dress had a white, knit rayon top with spaghetti straps and trimmed in the same small black and white checked taffeta of the attached skirt. My crown was constructed of flexible cardboard and sprayed with glitter.

While I found life in my small hometown rather quiet, the kids enjoyed their friendships and activities as much if not more than any other place they had lived. Even Skipper made a hit with the Landes' dachshund, and sired two beautiful, full-bred puppies. I gradually regained my strength, but it would be six more months before John came home. To fill time, I began writing a novel, and completed three chapters. The seed for my book, *Southern Winds A' Changing*, was planted in my head when I was fifteen years old.

The holiday seasons arrived, and we had John's parents and his bachelor uncle for Thanksgiving dinner. Then, I decorated for Christmas, but my heart wasn't in it. The kids were busy with friends, so I made phone calls to five or six couples to come for dessert and eggnog. Heaven help my soul if I had put a jigger of rum in the nog!

We got through the holidays, and it was coming up to April. I sold the house to a family living several doors down the street. They agreed to let us remain there until we left for John's next assignment.

At prom time, my handsome son took Robin, and Jerry took my pretty daughter.

My husband's long-awaited homecoming arrived, and I met him at the Texarkana airport sometime around his April birthday. He was home in time for Johnny's high school graduation in late May 1969. It was thrilling to have our son graduate from our school.

John had orders to Lockheed Aircraft in Los Angeles. For the first time in his military career, I refused to accompany him. Unwilling to take our kids back to California, my rebellion may have cost my husband the promotion to full colonel. John always claimed it was because he didn't get to attend the required military courses. Whatever the reason, I regretted he wasn't promoted, but not the concern for our children.

For the first time in his career, John used a friend's help to get his orders changed. He flew to the nation's capital, where Jack Kleuver assisted in his reassignment to the Army Materiel Command in Washington, D. C. The Kleuvers lived just across the District line in Camp Springs, Maryland. John bought our home on Easy Street in a new development near them.

Johnny sold his '46 Ford to Robin, and her parents bought our portable dishwasher. My son helped Robin start the first load of dishes. Our phone rang. "Mom, something is wrong with this dishwasher."

"I used it just before it was taken away. It worked then. What is it doing?"

"Foam is coming out everywhere."

"What detergent did you use?"

"We put regular dishwashing liquid in it. Like you wash by hand."

"Stop the machine. You must use detergent made especially for dishwashers."

We didn't hear anymore about the dishwasher, and it was the last boondoggle before the packers and moving van came, and we said farewell to hometown friends.

REACHING A TURNING POINT

We arrived south of Waldorf, Maryland in June 1969 without any thought of what the coming years might hold for us. We always lived close to the present, never thinking much beyond the next move and meeting new people. I didn't consider a time when our nest would be empty, or when we would move again, supposedly for the last time.

We took rooms in the Martha Washington Motel while interior work progressed on our Camp Springs home. It was to be finished by the time the moving van arrived.

Our house at 7230 Easy Street was two miles east of Andrews Air Force Base and carried a price tag of $37,000. "I don't think our ten-year-old furnishings will be suitable for such an *expensive* dwelling," I said.

John wasn't concerned about the furnishings.

The next morning, we rode north to have a first view of our new home. Turning off Old Branch Avenue onto Allentown Road, we came even with a fast food eatery. "Stop, Dad! Pull into the Burger King. I want to apply for a summer job." Lindsey had never held a job, but she hopped out of the car with apparent confidence and returned as an employee of the fast-food eatery.

Moving on, we pulled onto Easy Street, and there was our modified Dutch colonial. Pleased with my husband's selection, I walked around inside, imagining the arrangement of furniture, which I suspected *would fit* for the duration of our time there.

Within a few days, everything came together, and we drove back to Camp Springs to meet the moving van. Chris Jacobs, the girl from next door who was Lindsey's age, came out to meet us at the car. "Gosh," she said, "we're so glad you aren't 'blocks.'"

"What's a block?" one of ours asked.

Chris explained it was a term used for kids in vocational training. Those not referred to as blocks were called collegiates, perhaps because they were expected to be college bound.

The first evening, our four joined the two Jacobs girls, Chuck Bevard, and Louise and Betsy Novotny on the curb in front of the house. A tight-knit social group formed quickly. Chuck worked at Burger King, and he and Lindsey struck up a courtship right away. It lasted through her junior and senior years at Crossland High School.

The kids told me years later of the little clan's midnight rendezvousing. Chris Jacobs and the Novotny girls pecked on Johnny and Steve's downstairs bedroom window. The boys crawled out the window. Lindsey and David eased downstairs and waited for the air-conditioner to kick on, then slid the patio door open. All met on the curb in front of the house to talk about "life, philosophy, the war, peace and our dreams," Steve said. "That was a wonderful summer, and we were lucky to have those girls as our friends." He didn't mention the "t-ping" (toilet-tissue wrap) of another neighborhood group leader's house, but David told about it.

When a friend or two came over for each of our four, our den was a roomful of various ages. When school opened, Skipper and I had the house to our selves, but at the end of a school day and on weekends, there was a din of teenage laughter and loud music.

But it was our family that gathered there for the televised lunar landing on July 21.

Content with our split-level, four-bedroom brick, we settled in. Old wrought iron pieces went into the large downstairs den. Unfinished space on the lower floor showed promise for a fifth bedroom.

With our family housed, John reported for duty and bought a green 1970 Toyota Corolla to drive back and forth to the District.

Soon the house on our left reached completion, and was purchased by Bob and Jane Rice. He was a traveling chemical salesman. Their eldest son, Kevin, was away at West Point. The other three were Bob Jr., a high school senior; Ellen was David's age; and Sean under school age.

Summer ended, and Johnny prepared to leave for the University of Arkansas. His dad took him to Brandywine, Maryland to purchase a used car. They returned with a shiny black Volkswagen beetle. A dependable vehicle, I thought. We said goodbye to our first born, and I wondered if he felt uneasy about entering an unknown place, and making his way through college entrance on his own. It was the same feeling I had on his first day of school in Alabama, as I watched him trudge down the street with glances back.

Johnny left in late August, and at month's end, Lindsey entered Crossland High as a junior, and Steve as a sophomore. David began his freshman year at Taney Junior High. Lindsey drove a carload of kids to and from school in John's car on the days when he didn't drive for his car pool.

I was happy to be back on the East Coast, where so much of our country's history played out. Fall days enticed us to visit places of interest. On a beautiful Saturday, Bob Rice Jr. went with us to Gettysburg, Pennsylvania. The panoramic movie in the visitor's center set up the Civil War battle ground we later walked through, stopping at points to listen to recorded accounts of the fighting. The cemetery was evidence of a confrontational fury between North and South.

While we visited places of interest, I missed our son. When he went to California, worry dominated all thoughts. Now, I felt only five-sixths of a whole. One kid wasn't coming home to roost.

If Skipper could have spoken, he would have argued he was the fifth kid and I should feel six-sevenths whole. Like the kids, he adapted to his new neighborhood. It never seemed to matter to him where he was as long as it was with his family. Each morning as I loaded the dishwasher, Skipper sat nearby on the kitchen floor, and we had long conversations. The brown dots above his eyes danced up and down to my words.

Our dog took possession of Easy Street. He lay in the middle of it, waiting for someone to come home. Other residents accepted his claim to the byway, and eased around him.

Everyone in our neighborhood lived a busy life, and we all traveled in different circles. John worked with military and civilian types in the city. In Lewisville during his Vietnam tour, I had weaned from military involvement, so it wasn't a problem that his Test and Evaluation Division in AMC didn't provide a social base. I attended one meeting of the Andrews Air Force Wives Club to hear Art Buchwald, the cartoonist-author-columnist, speak, and never had any desire to be a member.

To satisfy a yen to write, I enrolled in the Writer's Digest Creative Writing Course and took up my novel where I left off in Lewisville. As the work progressed, I sent short segments for critiques under the working title, *Winds Blew From the South.*

John seldom went on frequent TDYs. He spent weekends designing and laying down a brick patio behind the house with the help of Steven and David.

Not long into Johnny's first semester, a letter came from one of his grandparents. He made two-hundred-mile-plus trips between Fayetteville and Lewisville to visit Robin, his girl friend. "He's wearing out his Volkswagen and isn't attending classes," the letter stated.

What should we do? Just allow the scene to play through? We did, and at the end of the semester, our son called. "I'm leaving college and coming to Maryland."

"No, you're paid in full through the term. Stay until the term ends." Perhaps I thought he would stop cutting classes.

After five years there seemed no end to the Vietnam War. Korea had taken my husband for a year. Vietnam claimed another year, and I knew he might have a second tour. In my mind, the war was unjustified. My judgment of it had nothing to do with John's vulnerability, or the performance of our fighting service men. I was among a growing public awakening about the war, which drained our country's finances, killed young men and seemed unwinable.

On May 4, 1970, the Ohio National Guard fired into a crowd of demonstrating Kent State University students, killing four and injuring nine.

Johnny, accused of Communistic leanings by one of his Lewisville teachers when he spoke against the war, called at the end of another wasted semester. "The engine in my VW is blown. I'm leaving it in Uncle Frank's driveway in Foreman and bringing Grandma and Grandpa Carroll to Maryland in their car."

Overjoyed with my parents' visit and having our son back with us, I nevertheless felt defeated in my desire for him to earn a degree. "Johnny, if and when you continue your education, you must pay for tuition and books, and show us that you're interested in learning. If you do that, then we will help pay your way."

He took a construction job and bought a ragged-looking old florist van to get back and forth. As is true of so many eldest in a family, and especially of boys, our son was having difficulty finding his niche. He created some of the problems himself, but much of it was because I expected too much of him.

People with whom he worked were not the most desirable associates. Red eyes and odor were clear indications that he smoked marijuana. I talked with him about unknown health damage from smoking pot, and lived in fear that he might be picked up by the police and hauled off to jail. "If you are going to smoke, please do it at home." There were times when I entered the house to be met by a distinct aroma emitting up the stairwell from his bedroom. I was grateful when in time he gave up the illegal plant.

In September, Lindsey entered her senior year at Crossland High School. Steve was a junior, and David a sophomore. Lindsey and Chuck continued as a twosome. Steve and Christy Koontz were thick as gravy, and David claimed Becky Mauldin, who lived across the street.

On December 23rd, Lindsey's birthday, Johnny worked around a pile of steel screens when they were pushed over and broke his ankle in three places. He lay in the Andrews AFB Malcolm Grow Medical

Center with his leg in traction. We took his gifts on Christmas Day and spent part of the holiday with him.

Before the accident, he had registered at Prince George's Community College. When released from the hospital, he hobbled on crutches to his classes.

I registered at PG, too, for an English class and Political Science 101, each worth three credit hours. At forty-two years of age and out of school for more than twenty years, I doubted my performance and ability to compete with younger students. To bolster confidence, I took the SAT tests and did well in everything but math. No surprise. I had failed high school geometry.

About this time, John entered the seven-month-long, bootstrap program the military offered. Taking night classes at George Washington University, he received his degree in the spring of 1971. He had missed Command and General Staff College because test pilots were needed to carry out test projects, but he did the C&GSC courses later by correspondence.

When school ended, Lindsey and David accompanied me on a trip to Arkansas. We made it to some place in Tennessee before our five-year-old Imperial showed its temper. I pulled to the side of Interstate 40, and David raised the hood. We stood in front of the car, wondering what to do next when highway workers stopped to assist. They removed the radiator cap, and steam spewed upward. The men drove ahead to a service station and requested a new water hose be delivered to us. In an hour's time, the hose was replaced, and we were underway again.

Before our visit ended, Mother and Dad agreed to return to Maryland with us. Dad had undergone prostate cancer surgery as we made our way to California in '63. Now, following many chemotherapy sessions and the probability that the cancer had metastasized in the bladder, he required frequent restroom stops. Mother feared he wouldn't make it in time, and every few miles on the return to Maryland, she asked, "Bennie, do you need to stop?"

We made slow progress on the first day, arriving in Nashville during rush hour. Interstate 40 wasn't completed in the Nashville area, which meant driving through the inner city to pick it up on the other side. Caught in creeping city traffic, the Imperial's temperature gauge light came on. I turned off the air conditioner, rolled down windows and plowed on, praying the car wouldn't stall on a busy street.

Somehow we made it through downtown and back to I-40. The gauge light still showed red, and I worried about damage to the engine. Back on the interstate, I drove the speed limit, and after a while the warning light disappeared. We rolled up the windows, turned on the air and made it to Lebanon, Tennessee, where we stayed the night and the car rested.

The next evening, we drove into Camp Springs.

We took Mom and Dad to many places. Dad tried not to give in to his problem, but at Mount Vernon, he was too weak to walk and waited on a bench. On another day at the nation's capitol, they walked through the hallways, reading names on office doors, while I stepped into Senator Fulbright's office for passes to visit the Senate in session. With passes in hand, we were directed into a small group to wait our turn to enter the loft of the Senate chamber.

Our turn was next when Dad needed a restroom. "Mom, stay here. I may not find you when you come out of the Senate room. I'll return for you and try to get us in another group."

We found a restroom, and I waited in the hall for Dad. When he exited, he was very tired. I took him to the Capitol rotunda, and found a seat for him. Returning for Mother, I passed all the groups waiting to visit the Senate, and knew we wouldn't get in that day. I found her waiting right where I'd left her. She and Dad always had an interest in politics, and she was disappointed.

Unable to continue going places, Dad stayed home with the kids while Mother and I traveled about. Before their weeklong visit ended, we convinced them to fly back to Arkansas. It was their first airplane ride. Later, Mom said she enjoyed it, but "Your dad was scared."

Johnny continued to work construction and detested it. His fellow toilers learned he spent time at the university and took classes at PG. They scoffed, "College boy."

John car-pooled to the District. For all but one day a week, Lindsey drove the Toyota to and from Crossland with a carload of kids. I didn't know until years later that on a Sunday afternoon she took her friends into D. C, and ran through two red lights on South Capitol Street.

Lindsey graduated in June 1971. The ceremony was held on Crossland's football field. She took an office job at a carpet company on Allentown Road, and planned to go to the University of Maryland in the fall.

While she worked, and the cooking, housecleaning and laundry for six people awaited me at home, I took several summer courses at PG. One day, fiberglass curtains from the rec room went into the washer with Lindsey's and my underwear. The next day in class, I itched, and squirmed, and wondered what caused it. At dinner, Lindsey complained, "I was miserable all day. Something caused me to itch and squirm at my desk all day." A light went on in my head when I opened the dryer.

During the summer, Johnny worked at a service station on the corner of Old Branch Avenue and Allentown Road in Camp Springs. He saved his money and went to Arkansas. In Texarkana, he purchased a BMW motorcycle.

Steven and David took summer jobs at the Andrews AFB golf course and skeet range.

When school opened in '71, they returned to Crossland. Steve was a senior, David, a junior.

During the holiday break in late December, I had a hysterectomy at Malcolm Grow Hospital on Andrew Air Force Base. After recovering, I resumed school at PG. One day, I drove into the carport, and Skipper set up a constant bark. Leaving the car, I saw he was upset with something underneath it. Bending, I saw a gray cattail dangling from the front under frame. Ellen Rice's dead cat was lodged under the hood.

When Ellen came from school, I walked next door to admit I had killed her cat. Chuck extricated her late pet and went with Lindsey to find a burial place.

Lindsey and her friend, Cindi Overby, rented a room on East West Highway, near the University of Maryland, and began the fall semester. She met Glenn Brack from Annapolis, and Chuck became part of her past.

After one semester, she came home and started at PG in January. Sometimes I passed her on the Beltway, when I was late getting away for my classes. She accused me of speeding.

Around this time, I began to think seriously about earning a degree. In education, I thought, despite a dream from childhood of being a Brenda Starr, the comic strip character. As a reporter, Brenda met interesting people, knew a little about a lot of things, and wrote about them.

I registered for four classes. Ann Beauregard and Alice Reitner were in my Spanish class, and we shared rides to PG for the next two semesters. Math was required to transfer to the University of Maryland, and I surprised myself by passing the course.

Johnny continued to work and take a night course at PG. He turned out beautiful metal and wood pieces on our patio. He had great admiration for Jerry Parsons, his sculpture teacher.

In November, my husband received orders for a second yearlong tour in Vietnam. He left in November 1971 to take up duty as commander of the Army Airfield at Vung Tau.

I had hours of study to keep my mind occupied, and four kids still living at home, all of whom were still capable of presenting surprises for me.

One day, I came from school to find a strand of cooked spaghetti hanging from the ceiling over the stove. Steve had made spaghetti. "If it stuck, it was *al dente*," he said.

If it wasn't the kids, it was the dog or some incident that left a memorable imprint. Such was the day when a call from the bank related that I was overdrawn. John had arranged for a sizeable allotment to be sent to our bank before he left for Vietnam. Unaware of a foul-up, I had paid all the bills by check. On the phone, I explained to the clerk that I would stop at the bank on the way home from classes.

I picked up Ann and Alice, drove to PG, and with a pounding headache, took an exam. Nausea left me unable to drive home. Ann took the wheel, and got us to the bank. She and Alice waited in the car, while inside I explained to the clerk that John was in Vietnam, and about the allotment. "The failure of allotment payments happens to a lot of wives whose husbands are overseas. I will hold your checks until you get it straightened out. Here is the phone number for the Army Finance Office."

At home, I called the finance office, and in a few days the money was in the bank.

There were no more money problems, and in June 1972, Steve graduated after a busy senior year at Crossland. He was the layout editor for his high school annual. His father was absent for the ceremony in the University of Maryland's Cole Field House. Steny Hoyer, then a Maryland junior senator, (now [2009] the U.S. House minority leader) was the keynote speaker.

In June 1972, I received an associate arts degree with honors from PG. The kids attended my graduation, and their pride in my accomplishment meant more than I had words to describe.

It was an unsettling time. Johnny hung posters of President Nixon and Vice President Spiro Agnew in the basement, and threw darts at them. In mid-June, the Watergate burglars were arrested. That development dominated Washington news channels, and with Carl Bernstein and Bob Woodruff's stories in *The Washington Post*, we had front row seats to unfolding criminal activity in the government.

Demonstrations against the Vietnam War, referred to as moratoriums on the war, increased around the country. They took place on the Mall, on college campuses, and across from the White House where Lafayette Park filled with protestors. Steven, David and I took part in one on the Mall when Rickie Havens was one of the performing musicians. All of us felt the war was ill-conceived and not worth the lives being sacrificed.

The biggest protest of all was scheduled for the summer week John came home from Vietnam for R&R. The kids and I planned to be at the Washington Monument for the event. Newscasts predicted a crowd in the triple thousands. My husband had never expressed what he felt about the war. We asked him to go with us, and to our astonishment, he agreed.

Arriving early, we gained a position not far from the tall grandstand. The Mall filled and music was loud. Speaker after speaker, young and old, famous and not-so-famous, criticized the Nixon administration for not ending the war. Helicopters flew overhead, filming the crowd and making John edgy. I felt for his discomfort, but I knew I participated in the work of a democracy.

Before my husband's week of R&R ended, we traded the '65 Imperial for a '73 Pontiac. I was reluctant to give up our old car, but there had been mechanical problems, and John thought I should have more reliable transportation in fast-moving traffic on the Beltway.

Back in Vietnam for another six months, he was deputy commander of the 34th General Support Group in Saigon, responsible for all Army aviation maintenance in the country.

Lindsey's friend, Cindi Overby, lived with us that summer after her parents moved out of state. One night Lindsey sneaked off to Someplace Else with another of her girlfriends. Cindi told me where she was, and I called the bar. With my daughter on the other end of the phone, I demanded, "Come home, now!"

"I can't. We are in my girlfriend's car, and I'm with her. Anyway, Mom, I'm almost twenty years old." Was I angrier with my only daughter for going to a bar, or because she aged beyond my control?

That summer, Steve worked for the House of Fabrics in Marlow Heights as a stock boy. He saved his money and bought a used white, TR250 Triumph convertible.

Summer moved along, and David, who would be a senior at Crossland in the fall, worked at the skeet range, and hung out with his friends.

Steve and Christy, still a twosome, were accepted at Lenior Rhyne University, a small liberal arts school in Hickory, North Carolina. When the fall semester opened, they rode to Hickory in Steve's Triumph, packed with school necessities to last a semester.

The next day, Christy's mother and I drove down with items that didn't fit in Steve's car. We unloaded at their dorms and took a motel room for the night. Surprise! Doris' husband showed up at the motel. The following day, she rode with him, and I returned to Maryland alone.

With Steven ensconced in North Carolina, Johnny became a full-time student at PG. Lindsey began her second year there, and I transferred credits to the University of Maryland and changed my degree goal.

Walter Cronkite was my hero, and journalism my aim. At UM, one of my professors assigned me to the *Precis* magazine, a university publication. I interviewed and wrote stories about interesting people on campus. The young students inspired me. Pantsuits were yet to become the national dress for women, and I envied girls in jeans sprawled on hall floors outside classrooms while I had to stand. Issue debates in Political Science class, enlightening lectures, and participation in campus demonstrations made school days exciting.

To keep up with housekeeping, shopping for food and making meals, I scheduled all my classes on two days a week.

In early November 1972, Richard Nixon was re-elected to the presidency. Later that month, John returned from Vietnam. Again, assigned to Army Materiel Command, Colonel Gary Boyle, chief of AMC's Aviation Office, requested him as the chief's assistant. He sold the green Toyota to Lindsey, and bought a tan Toyota Corona. My husband was on a health kick and soon had the kids eating bean sprouts, grown in a jar in the fridge, and drinking "tiger's" milk, a concoction he made that included wheat germ.

John may have thought he was past my foul-ups of earlier years, but he was in for yet another. Such as the day I returned from school, took chicken from the freezer to a sink of running water, picked up a book and went to the patio. Jane Rice walked over, and as we talked,

I noticed water streaming from beneath the bay window down the outside wall. After a lot of mopping, that evening, I had to tell John the water also ran down the fireplace wall in the rec room.

If I was distracted by a book and my neighbor, Nancy Boisey, a talented ballet dancer, caught Johnny's eye at PG. Her troop needed a male handler for the Christmas performance of *The Nutcracker*. Johnny met the need.

At the end of the '73 school term, David's high school graduation ceremony was held in the University of Maryland's Cole Field House. Then-Governor Marvin Mandel was the keynote speaker. That summer, our youngest son bought a 1967 BMW motorcycle. During the summer, he worked in construction with his brother, Johnny.

Steve came home from North Carolina. Finished with Lenior Rhyne, he took a summer job with a real estate agency in Camp Springs.

Sometime during the 1973 summer, I drove to Arkansas alone. For some time, I had researched my Carroll ancestors at the National Archives and Library of Congress. Dad led me to cemeteries where relatives were interred, and to his aging cousins for their remembrances. It was the start of many years of research in Virginia and North Carolina state archives and nearly every county courthouse in each state. Compiled information resulted in my books, *Carroll Frontiersmen, 1805-1987*, and *Virginia Carrolls and Their Neighbors: 1618-1800s*, published by Heritage Books, Inc., and a book titled *North Carolina Carrolls*. At this date (2009), the latter title is yet to be published.

Sometime during the year, Prince George's County tried to dispose of sludge built up at the White Plains Sewage Treatment Plant. A trial solution was to put the treated sludge—perhaps sanitized was a better word—on farmland. Mr. Jacobs, our Easy Street neighbor, decided to have it hauled to his lawn. A heavy rainstorm didn't help the situation, and the neighborhood endured a malodorous few weeks.

In the fall, Steve transferred to PG. His interest was in fine arts, and he and Joe Mayer, his art teacher, became fast friends. Johnny and David went to PG, as well. I never felt at ease with their ten-mile motorbike trips on the busy Beltway to get to the campus.

Before the university semester opened, Lindsey and I went to Woodward & Lothrop's, a large D. C. department store, to purchase her college wardrobe. She preferred mini skirts, and I liked something more modest. I never saw her wear one item we bought that day.

She and two other girls rented an apartment in College Park, twenty miles up the Beltway from Camp Springs. Our daughter worked as a waitress for her spending money. Glenn was at the university, too, and they continued dating. Occasionally, I ran into him on campus, but Lindsey and I had classes on different days.

Another term of school ended and on the Fourth of July, John parked the car in a Pentagon parking lot, and we walked a good distance to the place from which we could view the fireworks. When the display was over, we returned to the car to see the huge parking area surrounding the Pentagon filled to capacity. We were three o'clock in the morning leaving the lot, and had to drive fifteen miles back to Camp Springs. The fireworks weren't worth the walk or the traffic.

That summer Lindsey and I did fun things together. On a beautiful day, we went to Annapolis, had lunch and took a boat cruise under the Chesapeake Bay Bridge, and up the Severn River. Sharing adventures with her was a joy. We attracted strange people like insects to flypaper. They walked up to us and opened utterly unsolicited conversations. Sometimes they were worth listening to, and we didn't have to extract ourselves with kind words or excuses. If their talk headed out of the ballpark, we walked away with a giggle, calling them "our weirdos."

When summer ended, I started another semester at UM. One of my journalism professors apprenticed me to the *Montgomery Journal*, a weekly newspaper. I covered the Metropolitan Washington Transit Authority Board meetings. At the time, the board hashed out plans for the Washington subway system. I wrote articles around Metro issues that concerned Montgomery County. Lindsey often went with me to plays and dinner theater performances, and I wrote reviews for the paper. There again, like magic, we met our weirdos. We came to expect one wherever we were.

Soon after David entered PG, he answered an ad for a courier with the sheriff's office. Riding his motorcycle, he delivered parcels for a few weeks. One Saturday he sat at the kitchen table, having lunch with his dad and me. "I think I'm the bag man for the sheriff." Our son, whom some called "Silent," spoke only as our quiet one could. "I go to the sheriff's office, pick up these bags and drop them at different places. I don't know what's in the bags. It's real strange."

"Yep, you're probably a bag man, and you should quit as soon as possible," his dad said. David took his advice.

At the time, Watergate consumed people's thoughts in the nation. H. R. Halderman, President Nixon's chief of staff, was to testify before the Senate Watergate Committee. It threatened rain that day, and Lindsey and I arrived early with our umbrella at the Old Senate Office Building to assure a seat in the hearing room. Soon a sizable group waited on the steps for the doors to open. Pigeons perched on the building ledge just above our heads. We opened the umbrella to ward off their droppings.

About three hours later, we were among the first inside the hearing room. It was a fascinating experience to be at that history-making event. We were aware of only one celebrity in the room, Dick Cavett, of television fame.

It was around this time that John was sent to serve at the Federal Aviation Administration. This would be his last assignment before retirement. With him at work and the rest of us in school, we still passed like ships in the night. Before we could fathom it, the school year ended, and it was summer again.

Lindsey and Glenn worked the summer season of '74 in Ocean City's famous Phillips Crab House. They returned for the fall semester at the university, and rented at Seven Springs Village Apartments near the campus. Steve was ready to begin his first year at the university, and he shared the apartment with them. Lindsey continued to work as a waitress while attending UM, and Steve took a job at a bank. She laughed, and told about her brother's subsistence on small rations.

"Steve eats a small container of shrimp cocktail and a small portion of nuts. He measures out a precise amount of nuts each time," she said.

Our nest was down to four people and our dachshund. Skipper had aged to the state where he was unable to make the last few blocks on our walks. One of us picked him up and carried him. His weakness should have been a warning. One morning I woke to see him attempting to stand in his bed, and falling back. Alarmed, I roused John. We dressed quickly, and took him to the vet. The animal doctor asked us to leave him, saying he would call us later.

Around noon, the call came. "It's his heart. I can operate or put him down." We opted for the latter. John, Johnny and I rushed back to the clinic to say goodbye.

Our precious, fourteen-year-old Skipper died in 1974.

The loss of our pet wasn't the only sadness that summer. I had barely begun summer courses in Library Science and Journalism Editing, when Mother called. Dad was in the hospital again. She needed support, and I flew to Arkansas. I spent days in the hospital room with Dad and tried to study, hoping to pass the courses I'd barely begun. Mom spent day and night with him.

Six weeks later on August 5, 1974, my dad died. John and the kids drove down for the funeral. The day Dad was buried, Richard Nixon stood on a helicopter ramp on the White House lawn and waved goodbye to his friends, his former staff, and to the office of the presidency.

Leaving Mother alone, we returned to Maryland, and I arranged to take final exams for the two courses. I passed Journalism Editing but not Library Science. After several sessions with my instructor, and studying her handouts, she let me take the test again. I passed, and when the fall semester ended in December, I graduated from the university with a Journalism degree.

Meantime, David met Karen Jones, his future wife, in a Metaphysics class his second year at PG. Johnny and Nancy were still sweethearts, but he was destined to marry Andrea Hollomon after he graduated from UM.

In March 1975, John retired from FAA and military service. We searched in southern Maryland for property on which to build a house. An architect drew up our plans for the nineteen-acre plot in Charles County.

Lindsey graduated from UM in June 1975 with a degree in Sociology. In the fall, she and Glenn left for Utah. A door on his Mustang wouldn't close, and they pulled a loaded trailer. Glenn was scheduled to begin his master's at some university.

That summer, Johnny and David rode their motorcycles to Arkansas. While there, Johnny rode around a curve, struck gravel on the pavement and was thrown from his bike. One side of his helmet was shredded, but it saved his life. The front wheel of his vehicle was bent leaving his machine inoperable. Bruised, jarred and shocked, he rode the Trailway Bus back to Maryland.

David rode his motorcycle on to Iowa to visit Becky Mauldin.

When David returned, he and Johnny began the fall semester at the university. David moved to Bowie, and Johnny moved into an apartment with Steven in Riverdale, near the campus. Steve was in his senior year at UM, and still worked at the bank. Johnny hired on at Frank's Hardware.

David dropped out after finishing his first year at UM, but he promised me he would get his degree "some day." Johnny went on to get his degree in Industrial Arts from the University of Maryland. All of our kids worked and helped support their way through college.

In October, my husband took Johnny to Lewisville for his motorcycle. Repairs were made, and he rode the open-air machine back to Maryland in chilly fall weather with John following in the car.

Our home was completed in the last half of 1975, and we moved, we thought, for the last time on October 31st that year.

AFTER THOUGHTS

We led a life of travel, adventure and excitement, dimmed only by many separations for husband and wife, and a father from his children. After my twenty-five years as a military wife and John's thirty in service to our country, he retired. Our nest was empty, and we made what was thought to be our last move to Charles County, Maryland.

Looking back on those years, would I have made a marriage commitment? You bet, but it was best I didn't know the twist our life would take.

In the twenty-five years we lived in Charles County, many more fond family memories were stored. Sledding parties down the slope behind our house all the way to our two-acre pond. Fishing and picnicking at the pond. Trips with our children and grand children. Our daughter's wedding on our lawn.

Today, our clan numbers eighteen. Johnny graduated UM with a degree in Industrial Arts. He and Andrea live in Florida with our grown grandchildren, Brittany and Evan. Lindsey and Vance live in Maryland with Matthew, a high school senior. Grandson, Benjamin and wife, Kelli, live in Maryland with great-granddaughter, Rylee, and we have another great-granddaughter in the oven. Grandson Joseph lives in California, and granddaughter, Amanda, is a senior at Towson College in Baltimore. Steven graduated from UM with a Fine Arts degree, and married an artist, Anne Marchand. They live in Washington, D. C., and David and Karen live in Maryland.

All of our children are good solid citizens, and productive members of society. That's what I expected of them. I am proud of our family. Today, I imagine my four offspring saying, "Mom had a tendency to be over-protective and even a bit authoritarian."

Despite the hardships, John made a good life for us. Both of us thought we would live out our lives in Maryland, but once again a spirit of adventure enticed us. We sold our home in 2001, and now we enjoy life back in our home state.

LaVergne, TN USA
17 February 2010
173448LV00004BA/1/P